THE REFERENCE SHELF· VOLUME 46 NUMBER 6

THE CORPORATION
IN A
DEMOCRATIC SOCIETY

EDITED BY

EDWARD J. BANDER

THE H. W. WILSON COMPANY
NEW YORK   1975

THE REFERENCE SHELF

The books in this series contain reprints of articles, excerpts from books, and addresses on current issues and social trends in the United States and other countries. There are six separately bound numbers in each volume, all of which are generally published in the same calendar year. One number is a collection of recent speeches; each of the others is devoted to a single subject and gives background information and discussion from various points of view, concluding with a comprehensive bibliography. Books in the series may be purchased individually or on subscription.

Library of Congress Cataloging in Publication Data

Bander, Edward J   comp.
    The corporation in a democratic society.

    (The Reference shelf ; v. 46, no. 6)
    Bibliography: p.
    SUMMARY: A compilation of articles by different authors discussing the various aspects of a corporation, including its development, functions, responsibilities, authority, and the corporate conscience.

    1. Corporations--United States--Addresses, essays, lectures. 2. Industry--Social aspects--United States--Addresses, essays, lectures. [1. Corporations. 2. Industry--Social aspects] I. Title. II. Series.
HD2795.B25   338.7'4'0973   75-1164
ISBN 0-8242-0526-X

PREFACE

In Jean Giraudoux's play *The Madwoman of Chaillot*, the president of a corporation wants to tear up Paris to drill for oil. He pines: "I tell you, sir, the only safeguard of order and discipline in the modern world is a standardized worker with interchangeable parts. That would solve the entire problem of management. Here, the manager . . . And there—one composite drudge grunting and sweating all over the world. Just we two. Ah, how beautiful! How easy on the eyes! How restful for the conscience!" Of course, humanity is saved from this fate by the Madwoman. But one can read a good deal of criticism of corporations and infer that they are run by madmen, and one can read a good deal in the rebuttals of corporate executives to imply that they are being hounded by madmen.

It is the aim of this collection to provide some additional perspective on the problem of managerial responsibility. The corporation is part of the problem, part of the solution. We need its critics, we need its defenders, and we need an educated citizenry to get the kind of corporation it deserves.

What the corporation is, what it should be, and what it will become depends on an intermeshing of forces too complex to set out like an architectural drawing. What the editor has striven for is balance, common sense, and stimulation. It is hoped that this book will prompt its readers to give the problem of corporate responsibility their attention so that they will become part of the solution rather than add to the problem.

The editor would like to thank the authors, publishers, and agents whose permission to reprint material has made this book possible. He would also like to express his thanks to Professor Donald E. Schwartz of Georgetown University

Law Center for making available the material used in the course on corporate responsibility which he taught at New York University as a visiting professor and to Steven Bander, who proved invaluable in tracking down citations for the bibliography at the end of the book.

EDWARD J. BANDER

December 1974

CONTENTS

I. DEFENDERS AND CRITICS

EDITOR'S INTRODUCTION

This section attempts to put the corporation into perspective. The first selection, from a New York Stock Exchange publication, is as basic an explanation of how corporations function in practice as the Richard Goodwin excerpt which follows it is complex. These two selections point out, as the others amplify, that the responsibility of a corporation cannot be determined unless the terms are defined. Next follows a vigorous critic of the corporation, Melville J. Ulmer, who assesses John Kenneth Galbraith's view of the growing quasi-public status of corporations.

The last two articles offer some advice to corporations on how to remain viable. Manuel F. Cohen, formerly chairman of the Securities and Exchange Commission, suggests self-regulation while Irving Kristol chides American oil companies for reaping huge profits during the energy crisis of 1973-1974 without regard for public interest and public opinion—for "thinking economically" instead of "thinking politically."

THE CORPORATION AS A TYPE OF BUSINESS ORGANIZATION [1]

Sid Johnson had always been interested in radio and electronics. After graduating from school, he went to work in a printing plant. But Sid spent his spare time dabbling with hi-fi sets—experimenting with different combinations of parts made by various companies. Occasionally, he repaired friends' hi-fi and stereo sets. He also learned how to build cabinets which produced fine tone from inexpensive speakers.

[1] From *You and the Investment World*. 2d ed. New York Stock Exchange. 11 Wall St. New York 10005. '72. p 2-5. Reprinted by permission.

Sid's friends liked his sets so much they asked him to build sets for them. Demand for sets began to pile up. Sid decided to give up his job in the printing plant and go into the business of making and repairing hi-fi sets. He advertised in the local newspaper, calling his business Johnson's Hi-Fi House. Sid was the sole owner, or *proprietor*. He paid all expenses: for materials and equipment, rent for his small shop, taxes, advertising. The *profits*—the money left over after paying all expenses, including taxes—belonged to him and to no one else.

Business was good. In fact, Sid had to turn customers away. Nevertheless he felt his profits were not enough considering the long hours he worked. Sometimes he put in as many as twelve or thirteen hours a day, never less than nine. He gave up the repair end of the business to concentrate on making sets. Two years later he decided to form a *partnership* with George Gage, who provided enough money so that together they could build their own shop and buy labor-saving tools and machinery. Of course, they turned out more hi-fi sets than Sid alone could, and they divided both the expenses and profits.

The business continued to grow. In three years Sid and George could not keep up with the demand for their hi-fi sets, although they had employed six people to help assemble the sets and build the cabinets. The partners realized they would have to expand to keep up with the demand for their products and maybe increase their profits. Expansion would mean a larger plant, more machinery, tools and employees, including salesmen. Through their research efforts they had discovered how to build or assemble some parts—such as amplifiers and speakers—more cheaply and better than those they were buying from other manufacturers. This production, however, would require complicated and expensive machinery plus more workers.

The partners needed about $500,000 to expand, far more money than they could put up themselves or wanted to borrow. They decided the way to get the money was to let some other people become owners with them. So they set up the Johnson Gage Corporation under the laws of their state. Now they needed to get people to buy shares of ownership in their new *corporation*. These sharebuyers would provide the money for the expansion.

However, it would take a long time for Johnson and Gage to sell enough shares to individuals to raise the half million dollars. So they turned to an *investment banking firm*, one that specializes in raising money needed to start or expand businesses. Such money is called *capital*.

The investment bankers carefully investigated the new corporation. They decided it was sound and that its products would sell. So they paid cash for some of the *common stock* in the Johnson Gage Corporation. A total of 60,000 shares of stock represented the ownership of the corporation. Sid and George transferred their partnership business (including the factory, machinery, tools, customers and good will) to the new corporation for 10,000 shares of the stock. The bankers bought the remaining 50,000. (When an especially large block of stocks or bonds of a corporation are to be sold, several investment banking firms may work together. Such a group of investment banking firms is called a *syndicate*.)

The price of the newly issued stock was determined by the investment bankers and the Johnson Gage Corporation. Since $500,000 was needed, they decided to sell the 50,000 shares at a price of $10 per share to the investment bankers. However, they could have issued more stock, say, 500,000 shares and sold it at $1 per share.

After complying with Federal and state regulations relating to the sale of stock, the investment bankers sold the 50,000 shares to the public at a price slightly higher than $10 per share. This is the way the investment bankers make their profit. The process of having an investment banking firm buy stock of a corporation and then sell the stock later to the public is called *underwriting*.

The people who buy stock from investment bankers believe the company will prosper and as part owners they will therefore benefit. For instance, they hope that some of any profits may be divided among the shareowners as *dividends*. Or the shares of stock in the company may increase in value from $10 to perhaps $12 or even more, depending upon how successful the company becomes.

Since ownership of the corporation was now represented by 60,000 shares of stock, Sid and George with 10,000 shares owned 1/6 of the business:

$$\frac{10,000}{60,000} = \frac{1}{6}$$

Anyone with 100 shares would own 1/600 of the corporation.

With the Johnson Gage Corporation, as with any corporation, the ownership may be constantly changing as its stock is bought and sold by the public. The *marketability* of stock—the ease of buying and selling it—is important for any investor to consider. When a person buys a stock he likes to know that he can convert it to cash if necessary and advisable.

This is only *one* way small businesses can grow into large businesses—by changing from a proprietorship into a partnership and eventually into a corporation. There is, however, no set pattern. Sometimes businesses start as corporations with many shareowners supplying a lot of money, called *venture capital*. Such businesses are big right from the beginning.

This process of getting money from private individuals to finance businesses is an everyday practice in the United States. It is a basic feature of our capitalistic economic system. With this money, or capital, the corporation buys machinery, tools, and materials, builds factories, creates new jobs, and develops new products.

Who Operates a Corporation?

Obviously if there are thousands of shareowners in widely scattered points of the country, they cannot be expected to operate the business. So they elect a *board of direc-*

tors for this job. Generally, a board will vary in size from three members to twelve or more. These people get together periodically to make certain decisions about the business.

A board of directors makes overall plans for the corporation much in the same way that a board of education makes overall plans for a school system. Among other decisions, the directors decide how money is to be raised, how the company may expand, and what dividends, if any, will be paid to shareowners.

The directors also appoint the president, vice president and other principal officers to run the company. These officers in turn select the other employees.

Shareowners control corporations in which they own stock by exercising their right to vote—usually for the directors, but sometimes by a direct vote on company decisions. In most corporations each share of stock represents one vote. If a shareowner cannot attend the annual meeting, where voting takes place, he can give a written authorization to someone to represent him and vote his shares in the way he wants them voted at the shareowners' meeting. This is called *voting by proxy.*

How Many Corporations Are There?

꜡ In 1970 it was estimated there were about 1.6 million corporations in the United States. Some of these were "closed corporations," that is, they were owned by a small number of shareowners, perhaps members of the same family. "Outsiders" cannot buy stock in a closed corporation./ The Ford Motor Company, for example, was a closed corporation until early 1956 when, for the first time, some of its stock was offered for sale to the general public.

Some corporations are "publicly owned"—that is, their stocks can be bought by anybody with money to invest. In 1970 an estimated 31.6 million people owned shares in publicly held corporations. Some of these people owned as little as one share, while others owned hundreds, or thousands of shares.

Government Regulations

In the system of capitalism that operates in America, private individuals own and operate the corporations. But the government makes certain rules that must be observed. Primarily, the government's job is to help and protect. Rules and regulations made by our local, state and Federal governments are like stop-and-go lights. They are intended to help everybody, not just a few. An example is the Pure Food and Drug and Cosmetic Act. It seeks to protect the honest food, drug and cosmetic manufacturers from the competition of a few dishonest people selling food, drugs, or cosmetics that are impure or otherwise harmful. The same law seeks to protect you, the consumer, from these impure or harmful products.

Many laws and regulations deal with stock issues. For instance, most (but not all) large companies that want to sell their stock to the public must first file information about the company and its stock with the Securities and Exchange Commission (SEC). This is an agency of the Federal Government. The purpose of the SEC is to see that corporations that sell their stock to the public provide truthful information about the company and its securities for investors interested in its stock. This information helps the investor decide whether or not to purchase stock in the corporation. Registration of a stock with the SEC does *not* mean, however, that a stock is necessarily "a good buy."

Each state has certain requirements business people must meet before they can get a *charter* from the state government for a corporation. State requirements vary considerably.

The government's job is to help create an environment that encourages greater national productivity—more and better goods at lower costs for a greater number of people. But in a capitalistic economy like ours government is not expected to pass laws or regulations which threaten individual freedoms. Economic freedoms are as important as social or political freedoms. You should recognize that many laws governing our economy are controversial; that is, not everyone agrees that they are desirable. From time to time, some of these laws are changed, or repealed. New laws are enacted, as well.

Self-imposed regulations can go beyond governmental laws. For instance, the New York Stock Exchange has rules and regulations which are stricter in some cases than those passed by the government.

|' The growth of the corporation as a way of doing business has made it possible for millions of people to share the ownership of many American businesses. They also share the risks and rewards. . . . This development has been possible because of our capitalistic economy. /|

The fictional story of the Johnson Gage Corporation is an example of *capitalism*—sometimes called the "free enterprise system," the "individual enterprise system," or the "free economy." Under this system any person has the right to own and transfer property, start a business, make a profit, and work on a job of his own choice. In other words, control of economic activities rests primarily in the hands of private individuals like you and me. This kind of economy —capitalism, or free enterprise—has proved very successful in our country. For instance, the United States produces about one third of all goods and services the entire world produces, although it has only about one seventeenth of the world's population.

CORPORATIONS AND ECONOMIC BUREAUCRACY [2]

"Bureaucracy" is not a pejorative for unloved organizations. It designates a determinate structure and manner of

[2] Excerpt from *The American Condition* by Richard N. Goodwin. Doubleday. '74. p 215-20. Copyright © 1974 by Richard N. Goodwin. (Originally appeared in *The New Yorker*.) Used by permission of Doubleday & Company, Inc. The author, Washington bureau chief of *Rolling Stone* magazine, is a lawyer, writer, and former Government official and presidential adviser.

function—a process. At least two conditions are necessary to bureaucracy. It must, first, be relatively independent of the desires, special purposes or insanities of particular individuals, including the transient holders of supreme headship. Secondly, it must be large; large enough to permit and justify internal regulation through "policies," "procedures" and "standards," able to dilute and restrain the consequence of personality with the rule of law. Function and size thrive in mutual dependency, in inorganic analogy to soul and body, mind and matter. Once bureaucracy becomes a dominating form of organization, its attitudes and values are diffused through the society. In this way a single mind can become a bureaucracy.

Not all industries are bureaucracies, just the important ones. Of the more than one and a half million American corporations, one tenth of 1 percent possess more than 55 percent of all corporate assets—over one and one third trillion dollars. Even these figures churlishly understate the economic importance of the supercorps. Their behavior bounds the behavior of most smaller units, and all are implicated in their fate. Should even a single major American industry collapse—were that possible—it would be a far greater economic disaster for us than, say, the bankruptcy of Britain, the fall of France or the discovery that there was no gold at Fort Knox. (The last might be a relief.) Given the scale of the American economy, that is concentration enough to stagger the night thoughts of any nineteenth century Marxist. If this were really a concentration of capitalist wealth and power, the system would have collapsed into the state as Marx predicted. Let us rather describe it as a concentration of productive capacity.

Of course, one can also measure corporations by market value, revenues, profits, etc. It also makes a difference whether you include all corporations or just manufacturing corporations, thus excluding banks, insurance companies, etc.; although it would seem a little strange to neglect the holders of capital in an analysis of capitalism. But whatever method you choose the conclusion is the same—a concentration of dominant economic and productive capacity in a few large units. And the pace of concentration has been accelerating over the past decade.

The concentration would be even greater if we grouped companies according to shared interest and action, rather than by corporate charters. It makes more sense to think of the automotive industry as a single economic unit rather than as an industry dominated by three major companies. These companies produce essentially the same product in the same way. They never indulge in serious price warfare or technological competition. Their shareholders overlap— increasingly so with the growth of institutional investors— their managers are cut from the same pattern, they sign the same contract with the same union and prevail upon the same agencies of the same government. It does not take a trinitarian metaphysics to see that viewed from the perspective of social welfare or economic science, functionally, they are one.

The ideological justifications for economic competition are not metaphysical but functional: to vivify the economy by, for example, rewarding superior performance—innovation, efficiency and energy—and by permitting the purchaser maximum value for his money. Corporations are functionally distinct only when they are competitive, or at least when large elements of competition remain. Company names and corporate charters tell us only about economic history and the law, disguising the economic structure. In the world of the megacorporations there is little functional difference between monopoly and oligopoly—between telephones, computers, automobiles, steel and oil. Indeed, the oligopoly has the economic power of a monopoly without providing the same temptation to public regulation. For one corporation to absorb the others—to create a monopoly

—would bring great dangers and almost no advantages. Those who managed the takeover could not even be sure that their salaries would increase. Nor would stock necessarily be a better investment.

A functional analysis of the economy would expose a prodigious concentration of assets. We would see that the few corporations with more than half the assets are really only ten to twenty bureaucracies. We would also find that many smaller companies function as parts of the same structure. Such an analysis would require an exploration of actual differences in product, prices, innovation and the effort to expand a share of the market. Viewed this way we would find immense and accelerating concentration, already overflowing national borders. Any other kind of analysis is a study of names.

Who owns these economic brontosauri? Economic literature generally agrees that the managers are not owners. Yet, as we have defined ownership, managers do possess one of its attributes: the power to use and direct. (Somewhat qualified by the limiting authority of directors, etc. But those limitations are themselves the consequence of institutional structure.) Certainly no one else does. They are part owners, although their power has been greatly limited by its division from the other attributes of ownership.

Our search then turns to the legal "owners": the holders of common stock. More than thirty million people own stock in American companies. Many, perhaps a majority, hold shares in the larger companies. All of the economic bureaucracies have legions of shareholders. Corporate charters and corporation codes seem to agree that these shareholders own the company. Yet a shareholder cannot exchange his stock for an equivalent fraction of a corporation's assets. Neither can he demand an equivalent portion of corporate earnings; that is, he has no right to the value of the company. Yet ownership is a right to value; those without that right are not owners. If a security was, in fact, a claim to value of the company its price would tend to affect the present or rationally foreseeable assets or earnings of a company. It does not. For example, IBM with assets of around eleven billion dollars has a market value (total cost of all shares at the current price per share) of over forty-six billion dollars, while AT&T with over sixty billion dollars in assets has a market value of less than thirty billion. This is an extreme illustration of the fact that the market value of almost all large companies has no fixed relationship to its assets. And the same is true of earnings. A company like Xerox, with earnings of around two and a half billion dollars, has almost the same market value as General Electric with earnings of over ten billion dollars. Nor can any purchaser of stock in Xerox anticipate that its earnings will ever equal those of General Electric. These disproportions would only surprise one who assumed that a share of stock was actually a claim on the value of a corporation.

Forbes magazine says of market value that "there are few figures more ephemeral, more shifting, more dependent on matters that are frequently out of management's control." The nature of the securities market is such that the value of stock is as much a matter of metaphysics as industrial worth; more the product of alternating greed and timidity, passionate expectation and chilled detachment than of economic expansion and decline. There is some relationship between the value of securities and the strength of the corporation that issued them. Shares in a bankrupt company would be worthless. However, we need not analyze this relationship— analogous to the link between the value of the dollar and the strength of the economy—to establish that one who buys stock in an economic bureaucracy does not possess any fixed or proportionate claim to the value of that corporation as expressed in earnings or assets, present or future.

The fact that dividends are issued does not qualify this conclusion. After taxes and costs are deducted from corporate earnings, about 75 percent of what is left goes back into the corporation. This is known as the "cash flow," even though it doesn't flow anywhere. The remainder is for dividends, whose size is determined by management and not shareholders. Functionally, dividends are designed to help maintain a market giving shareholders some return on their capital. Shareholders receive less for their money than bondholders, but they are recompensed with hope.

Since shareholders have no right to the value of the corporation, they do not own it. If some Tibetan monk were moved to study our economy as a penitential exercise and was restricted to a volume containing the law of corporations, he might well conclude that shareholders did own them. He would discover that shareholders had a legal right to set policy, hire and fire managers, even to dissolve the company and distribute the assets. He would not understand that his studies were historical; the exploration of a legal structure which was the residue of a receding social reality. The broadening of stock ownership to large numbers of the general public has made it impossible for shareholders to exercise their legal powers. Ownership has been nullified through dispersion.

Some seem to believe it might be possible to organize shareholders, to reestablish shareholder power through unification. Among the many fatal barriers to this hope is the fact that stock in a particular company represents only a small fraction of the income or economic interest of most shareholders. They can neither hope nor afford to give that company the attention required by any sensible exercise of power. Moreover, if it were possible to organize shareholders they would be even more intent on short-term profit and growth than management. That is the nature of their interest. As shareholders, they do not represent the consuming interest, much less that of the entire citizenry. A shareholder democracy would be more rapacious, shortsighted and antisocial than an economic bureaucracy. However, such arguments are academic, for the ownership necessary to "shareholder power" no longer exists.

If shareholders do not own the company, what do they own? They own stock. In some fashion that stock is backed by the corporation. But, since their only right is to the value of that stock as determined by the market, stock is all that they own.

If the shareholders don't own the corporation, and if the managers don't own it, then who does? There seems to be only one remaining possibility. The corporation owns itself.

GALBRAITH'S THEORY OF MODERN CAPITALISM [3]

Piece by piece John Kenneth Galbraith has been building a general theory of modern capitalism as novel for its times, as comprehensive and nearly as iconoclastic as that of Karl Marx. Earlier components of the theory appeared in *American Capitalism: The Concept of Countervailing Power* (1952), *The Affluent Society* (1958) and *The New Industrial State* (1967). Now in *Economics and the Public Purpose* the elements are integrated, the diagnosis of contemporary economic ills is completed, and an ambitious prescription is suggested, including a heavy dose of socialism.

Worth emphasizing at the start is that Galbraith operates largely outside the template of orthodox economics, a notable renegade who has been continuously—and I think successfully—warring with the great majority of his more traditional colleagues. From the book-reading public he has received generous applause and lush royalties. The reactions from most of his fellow academicians have ranged from smirky smiles to angry outrage.

Galbraith is not in the fashion of the times a mathematical model builder or computer-doting econometrician, preoccupied with maximizing a hypothetical "utility function" in an imaginary world of perfect competition, perfect knowledge, perfectly equal opportunities and perfectly in-

[3] From "The Managerial Elite," a review of John Kenneth Galbraith's *Economics and the Public Purpose*, by Melville J. Ulmer, professor of economics, University of Maryland, and contributing editor, *New Republic*. *New Republic*. 169:24-6. O. 13, '73. Reprinted by permission.

stantaneous or "frictionless" mobility of resources. That is the orthodox economics of the academic establishment, and Galbraith (Harvard professor though he is) gleefully tramples on everything it holds dear, especially its reverence for the profit motive and market competition. As opposed to the abstract puzzle-solvers (like Paul Samuelson) most common in his profession, Galbraith is a workaday but realistic and extraordinarily gifted observer, keenly in search of the strategic factors that determine how the real world economy operates and what the consequences are of that operation. His canvas is so large that errant brush strokes are bound to be apparent to the delight of his conventional rivals. But for those with more interest in knowledge than in scoring a point, *Economics and the Public Purpose* may well go down as the most important book in this discipline since John Maynard Keynes' 1937 classic, *The General Theory of Employment, Interest, and Money.*

In place of the traditional, "impersonal" competitive forces of the market, the prime mover in Galbraith's portrait of modern capitalism is the managerial elite of the great corporations. Less than four hundred industrial corporations currently own three fourths of *all* assets employed in manufacturing in the United States. Concentration nearly as high prevails in most branches of finance, transportation, electric power, merchandising and mining. Guiding the nation's top thousand firms or so is what Galbraith calls the "technostructure," consisting of the "complex of scientists, engineers and technicians; of sales, advertising and marketing men; of public relations experts, lobbyists, lawyers and men with a specialized knowledge of the Washington bureaucracy and its manipulations; and of coordinators, managers and executives." It is their interests and objectives that comprise the most powerful single force shaping the country's economic decisions—its allocation of resources, the composition of its output, its technology, consumption habits, the form and manner of its governmental policies and, in some significant degree, its culture.

In orthodox economic literature, which includes virtually all university textbooks, reference is customarily made to the term "entrepreneur," the classic owner-manager of the business firm. The entrepreneur is buffeted by the forces of supply and demand over which he has no influence. Steadfastly, he strives to minimize costs and maximize profits. Even when textbooks recognize the existence of big corporate business, in the form of oligopoly or monopoly, the classic image of the lonely entrepreneur is revised only slightly. In its place is set the corporation's top management (or often just its president), which also strives to maximize profits within the constraints of the costs that it faces and the capricious demands of consumers, neither of which can it control. The great corporation, too, is subject to the discipline of competition, the trials and tests of the market. So goes the popular legend that commends itself to business leaders and also, conveniently, can be composed into the "publications" essential for academic promotions, fame and a modicum of fortune.

Galbraith presents an opposite view that discloses an aspect of business behavior that classical models overlook: the technostructure preoccupied with its own welfare. Stockholders by and large have no effective control over the firms they "own" and ordinarily no knowledge at all concerning their operations. In this era of complicated techniques even boards of directors are commonly at sea when specific, substantive business problems are raised. The momentous failure of the Penn Central, it is said, came as a greater surprise to its board of directors than it did to the president's office boy. The technostructure—the firm's bureaucracy of engineering, scientific, marketing, managerial and financial experts—represents the corporate brains, and its interest is primarily in growth and security: growth so that the corporate bureaucracy can prosper with a constantly expanding scope of activity, rising salaries, prompt promotions and always ascending prestige, responsibilities and personnel; security because growth is faster and more predictable when the strategic determining variables are safely under the corporation's bureaucratic control.

So through advertising and other forms of promotion the technostructure takes care of demand. Consumers are riveted so firmly to the need for deodorants, flashy cars, crackly breakfast cereals, electric dishwashers, color TVs and other symbols of affluence or conspicuous waste that some poorer families would rather go without food and medicine than resist the blandishments of Madison Avenue—and as the Census Bureau reports they sometimes do. As Galbraith sees it the giant corporations do not passively produce what consumers want (in accord with orthodox theory), but instead get consumers to want what they produce.

Further the corporations, for security and growth, must control costs, which they do by buying out or dominating smaller suppliers and by cultivating industry-wide and reasonably predictable contracts with labor unions. They must control prices, partly by shaping demand through massive advertising and partly by developing a peaceful modus vivendi to their mutual advantage with firms in the same or related industries. They must control government policies through close "symbiosis" with the Senate or House committees or the bureaucracies of the government departments or regulating agencies, that might affect them. They must control foreign trade, which they do by direct investments abroad, in the familiar multinational pattern and by surreptitious cooperation in cartels. In short the business of the giant corporations is not left to the whimsical trends of the market, of capricious consumer tastes or of political ideologies; all is painstakingly and effectively planned. Profits are required as a means to an end. A predictable and satisfactory flow of net income is essential for the technostructure so that growth can flourish and stockholders can be placated for the use of their money with adequate dividends and/or capital gains.

So successful is this "planning system" and so gluttonous are its appetites for the nation's resources that according to

Galbraith, it effectively starves the rest of the economy of output and income and cuts the nation's households off from some of their vital satisfactions. Within the planning system incomes are high, production efficient and abundant. Outside the realm of big business is what Galbraith calls the "market system"—some 12 million small firms, farms and many millions of service workers from repairmen to housecleaners. Here without the benefits of mass production techniques and often exploited in one way or another by the bargaining power of big business, efficiency and incomes stagnate; as in medical care, mass transportation, the arts and housing, output is also typically inadequate. In recognition of this disparity, he says, are the numerous and usually ineffective measures of government to redress the imbalance in aids to agriculture, cheap credit and technical assistance for small business, housing subsidies, price maintenance protection for retailers, Medicare, Medicaid, and so on. And of course outside the planning system, too, is government, deliberately downgraded and systematically used and abused by big business. Neither the environment nor the population's health can be preserved while such domination of government by business is allowed to prevail. Such observations lead the author to say that "in its mature form the (giant) corporation can be thought of as an instrument principally for perpetuating inequality."

In summary Galbraith faults the American economy for gross inequities, costly irrationalities, ridiculous extravagance in some sectors coupled with dangerous deprivation in others, all attributable to the arrogant, undemocratic, public-be-damned dominance of big business. His prescription for correction is many-sided and deals with a variety of specific issues such as environmental protection, inflation and poor relief. But his central and most significant proposal follows directly from his belief that the competitive market system of the United States has so grievously deteriorated that it is now beyond repair. He concludes that in a substantial part of the economy, the private, profit-seeking market must be replaced by a comprehensive system of governmental economic planning; that planning would entail public ownership and operation of the means of production—a "new socialism," Galbraith calls it, born of necessity rather than ideology.

Though cogent and persuasive Galbraith's analysis of the American economy, including his diagnosis of its ills, is not without faults. His interpretation of the big business "planning system" as rich and efficient and the market system as inefficient and poor, will not convince those of us who have recently paid bills to wealthy doctors or dentists or have seen the local building contractor pull away in his Mark IV or have observed the consummate skill with which so many "small" but flamboyantly affluent businessmen minimize their taxes. Nor can extreme inequalities in income distribution, as he would suggest, be attributed so simply to the planning system's exploitation of the remainder of the economy. Inequalities having little to do with social worth or solid contributions seem to be inherent in capitalism. They have prevailed wherever capitalism has, including some of the less developed countries whose only planning systems are the five-year plans regularly filed and forgotten by their governments. There are other difficulties with the Galbraithian model, but none, I think, that are irreparable. Its main lines are firm—more than that, incisive and germinal.

The weaker part of the book lies in its prescription. Here his effort in little more than 100 pages to cover policies in industrial organization, welfare, taxes, sex and race discrimination, economic stabilization, international finance, environmental control and political reform may be commended for its courage but not its judgment. His program for checking inflation while maintaining employment, for example, sketchily ignores structural problems in labor markets, producing large islands of joblessness that can only be met by specific government employment projects. Instead Galbraith places entire emphasis on fiscal policy plus selective price controls, a combination that has been tried and found wanting time and again in Western Europe and even, though half-heartedly I concede, in the United States. In countering inequalities he rests exclusively on guaranteed incomes, ignoring guaranteed jobs, focusing on the old, quixotic effort to reform the progressive income tax instead of exploring new and perhaps more promising ideas, such as a progressive and unavoidable tax on consumption. The need for public control of big business is acknowledged, but only vaguely described. Nowhere is mention made of the interesting "yardstick" principle, of public competition with private business, a proposal abortively introduced but never practiced in the New Deal. The point is not that all or *any* of Galbraith's proposals are wrong but that he does not devote the space and thought necessary for resolving the issues.

This sketchiness is most glaring in his central proposal for a "new socialism." Here he advances a socialism that "searches not for the positions of power in the economy but for the positions of weakness." As prime candidates for nationalization he cites particular industries where he believes the market has most blatantly failed: housing, health services and transportation. In another context he adds to this the defense industries and the very largest, or "most mature" of the nation's corporations either because of their overweening power or, in the defense industries, because the public is currently enjoying the costs though not the benefits of public ownership. Can American government, as it is now organized, run public corporations efficiently and progressively? Is the attempt even conceivable on any broad scale in the light of Galbraith's contention that business now controls government, rather than the other way around?

THE CORPORATION WITHIN THE COMMUNITY [4]

Detroit, like my town—Washington—has had a major riot. It knows the danger of frustrations within the community which seem to coalesce around a culprit referred to as the Establishment. The term appears to be abstract and elastic. In recent months, the Establishment has managed to encompass such diverse personalities as ... [Governor Ronald Reagan of California and Mayor Richard J. Daley of Chicago, President S. I. Hayakawa of San Francisco State College, officials of Dow Chemical Corporation and Patrick Cardinal O'Boyle of Washington]. It is the anathema of college student and black militant. For most of us it is a difficult and worrisome puzzle—who or what is this Establishment which is the cause of so much commotion?

A recent article in *Fortune,* intended to synthesize the views of two hundred student critics, has defined the Establishment as "the business, governmental, and academic power structure" which guides society. The students, as do some of their elders, give "big business" the distinction of being, to put it in the most favorable terms, the most influential institution in that power structure. The students appear to be of the view that technology has taken over our society; that it demands great size and a discipline that is dehumanizing and impersonal. We need to rethink the relationship between our institutions and the community. Both have made possible, in a manner never achieved before, personal and individual participation which seems inconsistent with the discipline and the organizational structures required by our complex social, political and industrial society.

The growth of the business corporation, in size and power, over the last thirty years has been tremendous. At

[4] From address delivered before the Economic Club of Detroit, January 27, 1969, by Manuel F. Cohen, then chairman of the Securities and Exchange Commission, now with a District of Columbia law firm. Reprinted by permission of the author.

the same time their number has tended to diminish. In every sense of the word, they are superorganizations.

Some corporate giants have such far-flung interests that no one man, or group of men, can hope to understand more than a fraction of their operations. Huge conglomerate companies have brought under one corporate umbrella many businesses in disparate industries, related only through control by multiple levels of corporate bureaucracy. Other institutions—governments, the universities and labor organizations—are also characterized by complex levels of organization. I suppose the concept of the Establishment is abstract because despite technology we are living in an increasingly abstract society.

Indeed, as I have noted, many feel that our institutions have grown so abstract and all powerful that they are no longer responsive to the needs or aspirations of mere people, but have developed a will of their own which is fundamentally hostile to individual freedom and self-fulfillment. This feeling of alienation has overflowed all too often into violence. The turmoil at the Chicago [Democratic party] Convention, the riots here in Detroit and in other cities and student rebellions across the land are manifestations of this struggle for the minds of men.

Of all the institutions I have mentioned, government is the only one specifically charged with promoting the welfare of the community. It must be recognized that, like every organization invested with important powers, government is not always free from abuse of power. Its leaders are not always men of good will, nor are they always endowed with such intellectual gifts as to see clearly the course which best promotes the public good. Individuals can, and sometimes have, used the "public good" merely as a facade to mask the misuse of power, sometimes with disastrous consequences for the community. But the important thing about our government, *as an institution,* is that it has built-in mechanisms to limit the misuse of power. The separation of powers and the checks and balances it makes possible, public elections and the requirements of procedural due process restrict the amount of power that any one man or group of men within government can exercise. The Constitution limits the authority of public officials to affect the private rights of individuals through governmental power.

Another check, is what I shall call "institutional criticism." Public policy decisions, for the most part, are made in the public arena. Our institutions, and our traditions, protect free analysis and criticism of public policies within the branches of government and in the press, professional journals and elsewhere. This device is bound up with the rather wholesome idea that anybody, no matter how clever, can make mistakes and can learn from the criticism of others. When that person is a public official whose actions affect others, he has a duty to listen carefully and to respond responsibly. I suppose what I am saying can be more simply put by the conviction that, in a democracy, institutions invested with political power must be nonauthoritarian.

It is still a staunchly held view of many that different rules operate in the private sector. Classical economic theory considers that competitive forces in a free market best insure an optimal allocation of resources. The idea of tens of thousands of individual producers and merchants making their own business decisions in a free market, with a minimum of government intervention, corresponded nicely with our democratic ideals of individual freedom and initiative. But the free market, as enunciated in classical theory, has undergone a revolution in this century—an organizational revolution, which has been accelerating rapidly since the end of World War II.

In 1932, . . . [Adolf A. Berle, Jr., and Gardiner C. Means] published their famous treatise, *The Modern Corporation and Private Property*. Its conclusions—so startling then— are commonplace today. It noted that ownership of productive property had been divorced from control. Ownership had become diffused among surprisingly large numbers of shareholders. The power which traditionally resided in ownership had become concentrated in the hands of a relatively few corporate managers who were all but immune from effective shareholder control. The shareholder's only practical recourse, if he did not like the decisions of management, was to sell his shares.

The tremendous growth and concentration of power in corporate organization has caused some rethinking and reshaping of the responsibilities of those who wield that power. The old distinction between the public and private sectors has been reconsidered and found to be wanting. Business leaders participate increasingly in government decisions and government officials in business decisions. Administrative agencies regulate important segments of industry. Many of our largest corporations depend on government contracts for their continued viability. John Kenneth Galbraith has termed this government-business partnership the "New Industrial State."

This fusion of government and business power to achieve social objectives is a political and economic fact of life. Traditionally, the function of business in this partnership has been viewed as the production of goods and services while the function of government was deemed to be the bare minimum necessary for the regulation of these productive activities to promote the common welfare. This view maintains the neat line between the public and private sectors drawn by the classical economists. Unfortunately it does not conform with reality. For as long as I have been in government, the government-business partnership has consisted principally in the accommodation of different interests and viewpoints. I doubt that it is realistic to single out either institution as the sole instrument of social and economic policy.

Some have seen in this government-business partnership the threat of a heavy-handed state authority dictating business decisions to private industry. I don't accept this view. As a member of one side of that partnership, I have witnessed the growth of a great industry beyond the dreams of its most optimistic members—the securities industry—under a system of cooperative regulation.

Others have warned of a threat coming from the opposite direction. President Eisenhower in his farewell message stated: "In the councils of government we must guard against the acquisition of unwarranted influence, whether sought or unsought, by the military-industrial complex. The potential for the disastrous rise of misplaced power exists and will persist."

Over thirty years ago Berle and Means made this chilling prophecy:

> The rise of the modern corporation has brought a concentration of economic power which can compete on equal terms with the modern state—economic power versus political power, each strong in its own field. The state seeks in some aspects to regulate the corporation, while the corporation, steadily becoming more powerful, makes every effort to avoid such regulation. Where its own interests are concerned, it even attempts to dominate the state. The future may see the economic organism, now typified by the corporation, not only on an equal plane with the state, but possibly even superseding it as the dominant form of social organization.

I am not prepared to accept this view either. I believe continued efficient and vigorous regulation not just by the various branches of government—but by industry as well—will provide an important check on the exercise of misdirected private economic power. But we must do more than to mouth such phrases if we are to bring back to effective participation in the important tasks ahead our brightest and most sensitive young men who, increasingly, feel alienated from our society, its leaders and its institutions.

The organizational revolution I mentioned has overtaken most of our principal institutions: our schools, our governments, our business corporations and our securities markets. The securities business in recent years has experienced a dramatic trend toward the combination of individual savings into a relatively small number of "institutional investors" in which a few fiduciaries make decisions to buy or sell securities on behalf of hundreds of thousands of small investors and others. This development has placed a great strain on our traditional market mechanisms. I don't know what this development portends for our securities markets or our economy. . . . But one thing is clear. Important powers are being delegated into the hands of a few.

Concentrated economic power transferred to a relatively few fiduciaries takes on the characteristics of political power. Large corporations (unlike tens of thousands of small entrepreneurs acting in a free market) have the power to affect a great many lives. Individuals are increasingly dependent upon membership and participation in organizations such as labor unions and business corporations to practice their trades or influence their working conditions. Doesn't such power carry with it the duty to act in full recognition of the responsibility of these corporations to all of society—to their suppliers, their employees, to the communities within which they operate, to the taxpayer and to the needs of the nation as a whole, as well as to their security holders?

The corporation has responsibility to the communities in which it resides, or in which its products will be used, not to pollute the air and the streams with industrial waste or to deface streets, public places and the countryside for commercial purposes.

The consumer has a right to expect that the goods he buys will be safe and reasonably well constructed. The sale of a defective automobile is not just a danger to the purchaser, it is a grave threat to every member of the community. It is surely an area in which the community has a legitimate interest. The sale of shoddy merchandise, misrepresentations and high-pressure sales techniques can have a tremendous adverse impact on the community, especially on the economically disadvantaged. As is so often the case, the persons least equipped to gather, or to insist upon, relevant information, to recognize the alternatives and to make informed decisions, are the most likely victims. The attorney general for the State of New York recently reported that 75 percent of all persons who complained of consumer fraud during 1968 were ghetto residents.

We have ample proof that such abuses create smoldering resentments which explode into violence, affecting the whole community. If further evidence of the responsibility of the business community is required, the past several years, a period of incomparable prosperity, have nevertheless spawned tragedy and violence on a scale that boggles the minds of those who believe that our civilization is an advanced one and that we share a common ethical and religious heritage. There can be little doubt of the political nature of the power of the business community.

It is to the credit of the business community that, in many instances, it has directed this power towards improving the lives of the disadvantaged and otherwise contributed to the attainment of accepted social goals. Job training programs for the unemployed and unskilled have created new hope. Construction of office buildings in urban ghettos has produced new job opportunities and scholarships sponsored by business have enabled many to leave the ghetto. Vast sums are made available to educational institutions serving those who do not fall into the category of the disadvantaged as well as those who do.

Professor Berle and the late Professor Merrick Dodd thirty years ago engaged in a debate—which has raged ever since—whether the state should have the sole responsibility for determining social policy or whether the corporation should share that responsibility. I doubt whether it is realistic to attempt any sharp distinctions between the public and private sectors. . . .

Whether or not corporate managers are motivated to maximize profits and whether, in consequence or in addition they seek to promote the social welfare, the important point is that the corporation *as an institution* is, in fact, invested with *political* powers.

The importance of this point has not been overlooked by the students interviewed by the *Fortune* editors or by other critics of the Establishment. Any totalitarian institution—public or private or semiprivate—can be run by well-meaning men; but the overwhelming fact remains—it is still a totalitarian institution. Our democratic ideals require that political power be limited; that countervailing power be maintained; that power be responsive to the community's needs and aspirations; and that legitimate power be nonauthoritarian. Adolf Berle concluded that corporate power was legitimate because it was generally accepted in the community. I suggest that the exercise of political power (whether by government or business) cannot be legitimate unless it is nonauthoritarian—that is, unless it is subject to free and systematic analysis and criticism—what I have termed "institutional criticism."

If we view the corporation as an institution invested with important political powers, some difficult questions arise. Do our traditional democratic ideals require that corporate power of a political nature be limited through mechanisms such as checks and balances, and the requirements of procedural and substantive due process? Should procedural guarantees such as the right to be heard, the right to confront witnesses, to cross-examine them and to present evidence be extended to employees of corporations and others directly affected by corporate actions? Many commentators argue that they should. Does the Constitution guarantee private rights to free speech and assembly against impairment by corporate action? The courts have begun to answer these questions in the affirmative. It has been suggested that the coming years will see the Supreme Court's emphasis on the protection of individual rights and liberties shift to defining the constitutional restrictions on the exercise of industrial power. Such a change of direction by the Court would mean a radical alteration of conventional legal notions about the private sector. It would also mean a recognition of the realities of our economic and political life.

These developments confirm the existence and power of the industrial state to which Mr. Berle and Mr. Galbraith have referred. Much of the pressure for judicial action in the corporate sphere, I believe, stems from a feeling that corporate power is not always "legitimate" in the sense I have used that term, that is, that corporate actions have a widespread effect on others and must be nonauthoritarian to be legitimate. They must be subject to free and systematic analysis and criticism.

To some extent, Federal regulatory agencies such as the Securities and Exchange Commission, the Federal Trade Commission and the National Labor Relations Board have provided this function. The *Silver* case a few years ago resulted in a decision against the [New York Stock Exchange]. The question raised by the parties arose under the antitrust statutes. The Supreme Court articulated its decision on the failure by the Exchange to accord to the plaintiff procedural due process. Corporate directors would be well advised to develop procedures of their own for institutional criticism of important corporate decisions, perhaps through internal review committees independent of on-line corporate decision making and, possibly, through public disclosure of proposed actions for review by segments of society and institutions outside the corporation, such as the press, community improvement organizations and organizations for the advancement of the underprivileged.

Those within industry need to hear all the competing arguments if they are to form a balanced judgment about their long-term interests, the interests of their industry and of the economy which gives them sustenance. Otherwise, they may only see a very narrow, often transient and quite possibly a self-defeating, view of self-interest. An example of industry self-regulation was the development by industry of its own safety and performance codes for certain products. While industry self-regulation of this sort is a necessary element for the "legitimate" exercise of power, it will serve its purpose only if it is rigorous, if it involves sacrifice and if it is available for meaningful analysis and criticism.

In the securities industry, with which I am most familiar, there is a well-developed structure of regulation by businessmen. The stock exchanges have greatly strengthened supervision of their members, their standards of conduct and other regulatory activities in the period since their rules first became subject to SEC scrutiny. When Congress determined to establish a system of regulation for the non-exchange markets, it authorized and encouraged the members of industry to form one or more associations to undertake a similar responsibility, subject again to SEC oversight. The National Association of Securities Dealers, which was established in response to this legislation, is charged with a part of the regulation of the diffused over-the-counter securities markets to ensure that they operate in the public interest. I do not wish to suggest that self-regulation has always worked well and in the best interests of the investing public and economy as a whole. Despite my disappointments, I am satisfied that it has been, and will continue to be, useful and helpful. Of course, these organizations need the full support of their memberships, a goal which they have not yet fully achieved. I hope they do because, although I am a regulator, I would feel more comfortable with less government regulation were I sure that the private sector would undertake the self-discipline which is not only necessary to the continued growth of our financial communities, and public confidence in them, but is also very clearly in the best interests of the industry itself. Unfortunately, the time is not yet. Perhaps, it will never be. Only a Pollyanna like me can still cherish the hope.

The individual business leader, no matter how clever or well-intentioned, does not always see all the consequences of his decisions. Like all of us in government, he is fallible, and can learn from others. He also has another very human characteristic. Like all of us, he doesn't always take kindly to criticism. That is why I stress the need for *institutionalized* procedures designed to protect and promote free analysis and criticism of business, as well as governmental, decisions as they affect the community. The press can help in the realization of this goal.

It has been said that the admirable man is the man with the courage of his convictions. Among those who hold great power, the truly admirable man is the man with the courage to question his convictions or, at the least, to allow others to do so.

THE CORPORATION AND THE DINOSAUR [5]

Every day, in every way, the large corporation looks more and more like a species of dinosaur on its lumbering way to extinction. The cultural and political environment becomes ever more hostile; natural adaptation becomes ever more difficult; possible modes of survival seem to be beyond its imaginative capacity.

That the cultural environment is hostile, is obvious enough. Today, businessmen, and especially corporate executives, are just about the only class of people which a television drama will feel free to cast as pure villains. Jews and blacks and teachers and journalists and social workers and politicians and trade union leaders and policemen—and just about everyone else—are given protective coloration on the television screen. Where one of them goes bad, there is sure to be a good one nearby, lest the viewers get the impression that it is proper to have a low opinion of the class as a whole. The business executive gets no such dramatic compensation. He is the only unadulterated bad guy. And since these programs are for the most part sponsored by large corporations, which regard them as suitable vehicles for advertising their products, the public is all the more encouraged to believe what it sees.

Among politicians, too, the businessman—and especially the corporate executive—has become the target of oppor-

[5] Reprint of article by Irving Kristol, Henry Luce Professor of Urban Values at New York University, co-editor of *The Public Interest*, and member of the *Wall Street Journal*'s board of contributors. *Wall Street Journal.* p 14. F. 14, '74. Reprinted with the permission of *The Wall Street Journal*, © Dow Jones & Company, Inc. 1974, and of the author.

tunity. True, there have always been politicians hostile to business, but they used to constitute a minority. Now, it takes a brave politician not to be hostile to business. If any United States senator has publicly denounced the scandalous way in which the oil companies have been made the whipping boys for the oil crisis, it has escaped my notice. And every attorney general, in every city and state, knows that his political future will be much enhanced if he announces an investigation into supposed "illegal practices" of large corporations. Most such investigations quietly peter out; but the headlines they engendered endure, and help shape popular opinion.

Painful Adaptation

Just why the climate has turned so hostile to business is a long and complicated story—about as long and complicated as the story of how the dinosaur's environment turned unfavorable to him. It suffices to say that, though it takes time for an institution to experience an environmental crisis, it takes only time. Yesterday it was the university; today it is the large corporation; tomorrow it will doubtless be the mammoth trade union. (In Great Britain, that tomorrow is today.) The question is not how to avoid such crises—they are inevitable—but how to cope with them. And coping means adaptation, *painful* adaptation. If it's not painful, that's a sure sign it's not adaptation.

But, even given an authentic willingness to adapt, one also has to have a sense of the nature of the crisis—otherwise one doesn't know how to adapt. And it is fairly clear that the American corporation today really doesn't understand what has happened to it in these past decades. It doesn't understand that, whereas the American democratic environment used to perceive it as being a merely economic institution, it now sees it as being to an equal degree a sociological and political institution, and demands that it behave as such. As is usual, in retrospect that change has an air of inevitability about it. A democracy is not likely to permit huge and powerful institutions, with multiple "spillover" effects on large sections of the population, to define their interests in a limited way or to go about pursuing them in a single-minded way. It insists that such institutions show a proper attentiveness to what is conceived to be, at any moment, "the public interest." Nor is it any kind of answer to say that, in the long run, the institution's single-mindedness will be for the good of all. In a democracy, large and powerful institutions, if they seek legitimacy in public opinion, must be visibly and currently attentive to the public interest.

In short, the large corporation used to be a single-purpose institution; an economic institution directed toward economic growth. It was very good at this job, would still be good at this job—but its very size and importance have resulted in its job assignment being changed. Small business can still be single-minded in its pursuit of profitability, just as small colleges can still be single-minded in their pursuit of education in the traditional way. But the large corporation, like the large university, impinges on too many people in too drastic a way. And so the executives of the large corporation, like the administrators of the large university, have to learn to govern, not simply to execute or administer. And to govern is to think politically, as well as economically or educationally. That is the price of bigness and power.

It will be asked: won't this have negative consequences for economic growth? Probably—and the corporations should say so. But if a democratic people prefer to sacrifice economic growth in favor of institutions which reassure them as to the reality of popular sovereignty, that is their prerogative. It is a dangerous illusion for the corporation to think that it is predestined by its nature to be an advocate of, and necessarily a propagandist for, economic growth and dynamic change at all costs. True, most corporate executives have an extraordinary aptitude for managing dynamic growth. But in the "natural" environment of today, that aptitude could lead to extinction of the species.

The difference between "thinking economically" and "thinking politically" is enormous. "Thinking economically" means trying to discern the opportunity that every problem gives rise to. "Thinking politically" means trying to discern the problem that every opportunity gives rise to. The transition from the one to the other is bound to be difficult.

Thus, one wonders what happened in the boardrooms of the major oil companies when those lovely fourth-quarter profits began to roll in. These profits, after all, were directly connected with the hardship, inconvenience and discomfort then being experienced by the American people. Did the directors and top executives sit around gloomily, muttering: "O Lord, we've got a terrible problem on our hands. What on earth can we do?" This may have been the case with one or two companies, but it obviously did not happen in the main, since nothing was done to cope with the problem. Nothing, that is, except for the preparation of a few press releases containing specious and self-serving arguments.

One such specious argument was to the effect that this new profitability merely brought the return on capital for the oil companies up to the average of all manufacturing companies. This is true—but what kind of argument is it? For all corporations to claim a "right" to an average return on capital is rather like all Americans claiming a "right" to the average family income, or all employees of oil companies claiming a "right" to the average wage for the industry. There is no such "right" and only a fanatical egalitarian would imagine it. Corporate executives are not ordinarily such egalitarians—but apparently they are capable of thinking that way, given sufficient temptation.

Another specious argument was to the effect that most of these swollen profits would be reinvested in the search for oil, the construction of new refineries, etc. Once again, this argument is true—but, once again, what kind of argument is it? One needn't be a left-wing economist to perceive that such a reinvestment of capital would ultimately result in enriching the company (and its stockholders, and its stock-holding executives) by increasing its assets. And yet, in their publicity, the oil companies point to this intention as evidence of their public-spiritedness, pure and simple.

Some Suggestions

Had the oil companies been "thinking politically," there were many things they could have done—some small, some big, all reassuring to the public. For instance, why didn't it occur to one of the companies to announce that, despite these profits, it would declare no increase in dividends or in executive salaries this year? It might not have helped much, but it could have helped a little. In a bolder vein, why shouldn't the oil companies have simply decided that they couldn't *afford* such large profits, in these circumstances? They then could have set the price of oil at a level which would have produced a 15 percent or 20 percent increase in profits, instead of the more spectacular percentages that made the headlines. This would not really have helped the consumer much—not more than a few pennies, one is told—but it would have helped the oil companies a great deal.

The reason, presumably, that the oil companies did not do this was because they wanted to raise the capital necessary to do "their job." But no large corporation today is free to define its "job" as it sees fit. Had the oil companies been "thinking politically," they would have realized that they had another and more responsible task—securing the trust and confidence and good will of the public. And this second mission, since it is the precondition of survival, must have priority over the first. As it is, the price for "thinking economically" is now being paid. The oil companies will, in the end, surrender a large portion of their profits while shouldering a full portion of public obloquy. Meanwhile *all* American corporations have lost some of their credit with the public.

II. VIEWS ON CORPORATE RESPONSIBILITY

EDITOR'S INTRODUCTION

Corporate responsibility takes many shapes and forms. Environmental and consumer groups give it a broad interpretation which is anathema to those who believe that corporate responsibility consists simply of staying in business. It is a complicated problem requiring an understanding of law, politics, economics—and an ability to forecast events.

The opening selection, a debate between Eli Goldston and Milton Friedman, is a classic presentation of the overall conflict. Next, David Packard suggests that corporate giving to universities is not done for altruistic purposes but to further the ends of a business-oriented society. On the other hand, Phillip Blumberg asks the corporation to transcend its immediate goals and recognize its responsibility to correct environmental harm. The New York *Times* article that follows illustrates the tactics employed to force corporations to become "responsible": suits against corporations from within and without, withdrawals by universities of their portfolios from "misbehaving" corporations, and so on. But thrust is followed by counterthrust. A *Fortune* article shows how corporations must fight back to survive. The concluding article by Martin Lipton on English company law shows that the problem is not exclusively American.

SOCIAL RESPONSIBILITY AND CORPORATE POLICY MAKING [1]

FRIEDMAN: What a corporate executive is really promoting are the interests of his stockholders. He's an employee

[1] Reprint of "The 'Responsible' Corporation: Benefactor or Monopolist?" excerpts from a debate between Milton Friedman, professor of economics, University of Chicago, and the late Eli Goldston, chairman of the board of Eastern Gas & Fuel Associates. *Fortune.* 88:56. N. '73. Reprinted by permission. The debate opened a three-day conference of business executives held in New York City in October 1973.

of the stockholders, and profit is a shorthand term for the interests of his stockholders. Henry Ford, for example, in pursuit of his own profit, benefited the public, brought in methods of mass production, higher wages. Did he do this because he wanted to promote social goals? In his private capacity he pursued his social goals; he financed the Dearborn *Independent*, an anti-Semitic newspaper. Henry Ford's notion of what was socially responsible was promoting anti-Semitism. . . . Are you really willing to have executives decide what are social goals? I am not.

A really competitive enterprise can't sacrifice profit to social goals or else it will go out of business. It seems to me that the corporate executive who stands up in public and states, "My corporation is pursuing socially responsible goals at the expense of profit," should be a prime candidate for antitrust action, because he cannot do that unless he has some monopolistic power.

GOLDSTON: We took a poll of our shareholders and we found a rather remarkable attitude. They didn't want us to maximize profits. We said we're giving 1 percent of our pretax income away in charitable contributions, and 87 percent of them stood up and cheered.

It's difficult to know how to maximize profits anyway. In the real business world you're lucky if you've got a plus or minus 10 percent fix on things.

A corporation is its people and they are not detached from society, which has come to expect corporations to do something more than maximize. . . . It all boils down to whether large publicly held corporations are social aggregations of talent that can be used by a wise government—paying attention to the fact that corporations must make a profit, but not a maximum profit—to accomplish social good.

FRIEDMAN: The best way corporations can be used to accomplish social goals is (a) by forcing them to compete so they don't have these monopolistic profits to throw around and (*b*) by setting up rules so they've got to pay for resources they use and charge for the goods they distribute. When water is scarce it ought to be highly priced, and it's appropriate for the government to impose water taxes and require corporations, in maximizing profits, to take into account those costs. But will you tell me how we go from that to the proposition that corporations have executives who can be trusted to use the funds of their shareholders, employees, or customers to accomplish these wise social goals?

GOLDSTON: It's probably a good thing in any democratic society to have a multiplicity of decision makers—even if you take a scattering of not-so-bright and awfully conservative and somewhat eccentric executives. There's going to be five thousand of them, each with a little pot of money to do something with. I'd sooner have them than Congress if what I was looking for was a multiplicity of imaginative ventures. . . . And it is the multiplicity of decision spots that creates a wonderful opportunity for innovation and change. . . .

The great danger of this harping on maximization is that it lets the cheapest louse in every operation say what's good for the country. . . . You can't let the lowest common denominator in American industry seize upon an antique philosophy and use that to justify resistance to corporate participation in moving forward a country that all of us are going to be living in. And the corporation is going to be living long after the management is gone.

FRIEDMAN: There speaks the classical cartelizer!

I think social change should take place through individuals pursuing values they believe in—with *their own* money. You've got no right to spend somebody else's. . . . I think we need an Eleventh Commandment: Thou shall do good at your own expense.

CORPORATE SUPPORT OF PRIVATE
UNIVERSITIES [2]

The subject of corporations and the private universities is one I have been interested in over a number of years. I have been on the giving end as a corporation executive—and, for nearly two decades, on the receiving end as a university trustee. I tell you this, not to claim any special wisdom on the subject, but rather to point out that I was involved both before and during the turmoil of the late 1960s and that my views are somewhat modified over those I held in the 1950s. I am no longer a university trustee, which perhaps should make me more objective—but I am still strongly devoted to the cause of the private university because I believe it to be an institution of tremendous importance in our society. It is an institution not only with a distinguished tradition, but one that has a vital role for the future welfare and progress of our country.

The legal justification for contributions of corporate funds to educational institutions had been established in 1953 in a New Jersey case—*A. P. Smith Manufacturing Company v. Barlow, et al.* And the tax deductibility was first established for such contributions by the Internal Revenue Code of 1939, and later superseded by Section 170 of the 1954 Internal Revenue Code.

Over many years, the practice of business support for education had developed along a number of lines. For example, it was well accepted for business and industry to support research in a field of particular interest. There was no problem in contributing funds for a specific research project of importance to the firm. This practice was followed long before the *A. P. Smith* decision in 1953.

Scholarships for employees, or for their children, provided another contributory mechanism.

[2] From article by David Packard, chairman of the board, Hewlett-Packard Company. The article was adapted from a speech before the Committee for Corporate Support of American Universities, October 17, 1973. *Financial Executive.* 42:30-5. Mr. '74. Reprinted by permission.

In addition, many companies found it appropriate to support a university or college located in the geographical area of its headquarters or at one of its major plant locations, as an act of goodwill and good corporate citizenship.

By the late 1950s, then, corporate support of education —in one form or another—had become reasonably common, reasonably well accepted by stockholders, and generally expected by the general public—at least by those who were college and university graduates. Estimates of the amount of corporate money going to colleges and universities throughout America in 1958 was in the range of $10 million.

Thus, there was broad and increasing corporate support for higher education, but could a special case be made for the major private universities? This was the challenge that faced the Committee for Corporate Support of American Universities when it was formed some fifteen years ago.

It was quickly apparent that one of the first problems to be encountered would be to decide which universities should be included on the recommended list. Deliberations on this question brought about some guidelines which were carefully thought out. With one exception, which I will discuss in more detail, the guidelines have stood the test of time very well.

The first guideline was that the university to be supported should be a private university, not a state-supported school. It was recognized that many state universities met the same standards of excellence as the leading private universities, but corporations were already doing their part through payment of taxes and should not be expected to provide additional support. There might be exceptions, but this was the general rule.

Second, the private university to be supported should have graduate schools of distinction covering a broad range of studies. Graduate schools were considered especially important to corporations for four reasons:

They were a major source of professional people who would be needed by the corporation.

They were the centers of important research.

They were a major source of the Ph.D.'s and professors for all levels of higher education in America and their influence was thus greatly magnified.

A fourth reason was that these major private universities gave important leadership to all of higher education in America in terms of educational policy and behavior as well as in knowledge and in men and women to fill the professorial chairs. These were the "bell cow" universities, and the lesser institutions all across the country would do well to follow the lead of these distinguished institutions. Corporations, by supporting these "bell cow" universities, could help raise the standards of all the colleges and universities in America, a role clearly well justified for the corporate dollar.

In offering these guidelines for corporate support of private universities, the committee was careful to add three other stipulations.

One was that the aid to these select private universities should be over and above what the corporation was already doing for education. The other was that the corporation should select the recipients for support and give the money directly to the universities, not through the committee. A list of universities which the committee believed qualified under the guidelines was provided, but the committee was always careful to emphasize the guidelines and respect the judgment of the corporate officers in their selection of specific institutions.

The committee recommended that the amount given to any of the universities should be substantial, and that it should be continued over a period of years. This would make contributions under the program much more useful to a university than large random contributions or insignificant continuing contributions.

The committee also recommended that the corporate

gifts to these universities should have no restrictions on the use of the funds.

I feel the committee made a good case for the major private universities. That case stands well today, and it will continue to be a valid and important basis for continuing corporate support of these institutions. In fact, in reading Arthur H. Dean's statement of August 1970, for the Committee for Corporate Support of American Universities, I find that the policies and guidelines which were established in the early years are still in effect—and with one exception I commend them to you as a sound program for the future.

The only exception I would make is the guideline stating that corporate funds given to private universities should be unrestricted in their use by the university.

I supported that proposition ten years ago because I, like the other members of the committee, was a university trustee—and I thought trustees knew best how a corporate contribution should be used and that trustees had substantial control over how funds were used. In retrospect, that point was probably debatable then. It seems to me that it is even more so today.

I recognize that for the university, unrestricted money is most valuable. It allows the trustees, or the administration, or the faculty to undertake programs which might otherwise not attract financial support from the outside. It does not necessarily follow, however, that unrestricted money, used as it has been used, is always in the interest of the corporation. That, however, is precisely what the corporate officer considering a contribution to a university should be thinking about. Should our corporations make an unrestricted contribution and leave it to the trustees or the administration or the faculty to decide how the money should be used, or do we have a responsibility to our stockholders to be sure the money contributed will, in some defensible way, benefit our corporation?

Fifteen or twenty years ago the trustees of the major private universities could and did play a role in university policy. Most trustees were also corporate officers. It is quite understandable then that we all felt comfortable in recommending that corporate funds be unrestricted.

The situation is vastly different today. Almost every board of trustees must have its members selected from a wide array of constituents: students, faculty, alumni, various ethnic groups, etc. Moreover, much of the power has gone to the faculty, and too often faculty decisions are determined by a militant minority of the faculty.

All this may be good for our private universities. I do not believe so. I believe the case for a corporation giving unrestricted funds to a private university can no longer be supported.

Let's go back and look at some of the guidelines on which the case for corporate support of these private universities has been based.

First, we have said these universities are a major source of the professional people our corporations will need for their future growth and progress. The problem with the unrestricted gift here is that it is not likely to be used to help a professional school. The Graduate School of Business at Stanford receives no funds from unrestricted gifts. The only way a corporation can support this distinguished school is by giving funds designated specifically for the school. I believe the same situation prevails for the Harvard Business School and most of the other great business schools around the country.

The practice varies from university to university and may vary among the professional schools in a given university. To the extent a corporate contribution is to be justified on the basis that it helps assure a continuing supply of professional people, the funds must be designated specifically for the professional schools you want to support if you want to be certain.

A second premise to justify corporate support for universities is that they are in the business of generating new knowledge through research. Here again, very little unrestricted money is directed to support the many excellent research programs one finds at our private universities. Most of the research at these universities is supported by the government or by large foundations. I happen to believe these universities would be better off if more of their research was supported by business and less by the government. If you should happen to agree, take time to find an area of research you believe to be important to your company, and support it on a specific basis.

On this point you may find some research in the field of the social sciences or the humanities which will be relevant to your business. In this area some good two-way communication could be most helpful, and I believe more corporate dollars specifically designated just might open up the kind of communication we sorely need.

The third guideline has to do with the fact that these major universities are an important source of professors for all of higher education. This is of course true, and this greatly magnifies the impact of these great private schools.

Because of this magnifying factor I believe the corporate executive has a double responsibility to make sure his dollars are constructive rather than destructive—and there is no way to do this with unrestricted money.

Let me give you just one example of what did happen in the late 1960s.

Professor Richard Flacks, who was a top intellectual figure in the Students for a Democratic Society, said this in 1969:

Data on the distribution of student protest on American campuses quite clearly shows that the student movement had its origins at the highest quality state universities and prestigious private universities and colleges, that the movement continues to have its widest following on such campuses, and that it has only recently spread to schools of lower prestige and quality.

If you want to be sure your funds do not have this kind of multiplying effect, restrict them to those areas you believe are educating the right kind of professors.

The fourth premise, and the only one so far which might possibly be used to justify unrestricted corporate gifts, is that the great private universities give distinctive leadership to all of higher education in America—the "bell cow" theory. This premise sounded very convincing to me in 1959. In 1973 I'm much less sure.

Is kicking ROTC programs off the campus the kind of leadership we need?

Is prohibiting business from recruiting on the campus the kind of leadership we need?

Should these universities serve as haven for radicals who want to destroy the free enterprise system?

Should students be taught that American corporations are evil and deserve to be brought under government control?

Should a board of trustees sit as sole judge of the social responsibility of each American corporation—and use this as a basis for deciding whether its stock should be held in the university portfolio?

Fortunately, most of the colleges and universities over this great country of ours have not blindly followed the lead of some of the "bell cows" we touted ten or fifteen years ago.

Clearly, unrestricted corporate contributions cannot be justified.

Some who argue for unrestricted grants will say that universities should be isolated, "ivory tower" centers of learning outside the affairs of the world. There may be something to this position—let's look at it.

These same people like to call a university a community of scholars which, of course, it should be. In a university these scholars are grouped together in schools and departments. Sometimes we find groupings of scholars within the university who are hostile to business and the free enterprise system. All too often these groupings tend to perpetuate themselves because they attract professors in the same mold. Departments of economics are particularly vulnerable, as are departments of religion and other areas of the humanities. I happen to believe that such hostile groups of scholars are, to a large degree, responsible for the antibusiness bias of many of our young people today. And I do not believe it is in the corporate interest to support them—which is what we do to a greater or a lesser degree with unrestricted funds.

I believe we will do more in the interest of our corporations and just as much for the universities by being specific in designating where our funds go.

A university is strong to the extent its schools and departments are strong. In the future, let's focus our money and our energy on those schools and departments which are strong and which also contribute in some specific way to our individual companies, or to the general welfare of our free enterprise system. On this basis, more support for these great private universities can be justified. I commend this to you as a wise and productive basis for future corporate policy in relation to the major private universities of America.

CORPORATE RESPONSIBILITY AND ENVIRONMENTAL ABUSE [3]

At the outset of our discussion of corporate responsibility and environmental abuse, it is desirable to inquire what we mean when we refer to corporate responsibility. This concept is a philosophy of business enunciated by leaders of major American enterprise including Owen D. Young in the 1920s, Frank Abrams in the 1950s, and innumerable others in the years since—a philosophy that business must serve its employees, customers, suppliers, and the American society generally, as well as its shareholders, that business is too important a factor in society to confine its objectives to making as much money as possible for its shareholders.

[3] From introductory statement by Phillip I. Blumberg, dean, University of Connecticut School of Law, at the Association of American Law Schools Round Table, Chicago, December 29, 1970. Reprinted by permission of the author.

Corporate responsibility, as expressed in this fashion, has been evidenced by highly welcomed business support for charities, for education, for the arts, for employment of minority groups, for efforts to deal with poverty, race relations, and urban problems, and for other social objectives commanding an overwhelming consensus of public approval. . . .

In the nonenvironmental area, the . . . question is not the fact of the recognition by business of corporate social responsibility but whether the public acceptance-expectation-demand process will increase in intensity so that the voluntary nature of business response will be progressively restricted and the funds allocated to this area as a result of public demand—funds which will then for practical purposes be involuntary social costs of doing business—increase to a level nearer the tax-deductible ceiling. The role businessmen themselves play in this process of acknowledgment and acceptance of such social costs may well have significant influence on the future place of business in the society. . . .

When we turn from the traditional areas of corporate social responsibility to the field of the environment, the question arises whether such a development may not already have occurred and whether the public acceptance-expectation-demand process has not already reached such a level of intensity that business has lost much of its freedom of choice.

The dynamics of the intensification of public expectation and demand in the environmental field have been marked by at least three new major elements not included in the factors which have led in the past to the development of corporate responsibility in the social sphere. This marks out the area as novel and helps explain why the pressures of the public for corrective action have reached such overwhelming proportions.

In the first place, the consequences of environmental abuse are faced directly by all members of the community, and the public is aroused to an extent never experienced in the more traditional areas of social responsibility. The problem presented by environmental abuse affecting the community as a whole is radically different from the concern that an individual not directly affected by a social problem may feel for those who are affected and for the impact that such social problems affecting others may have on the community as a whole. Thus, the considerations presented by smog in a community which affects every resident directly and from which he cannot escape are plainly different from the considerations involved in the evaluation by a middle-class white of his response to such community problems as employment opportunities for disadvantaged minority groups. The entire community, not a limited social group, is the victim.

Secondly, in the environmental area, business is being called upon to help solve problems which it has itself created. There is no question as to the individual responsibility of the plant for the air or water pollution which it is causing in the community. The business is not sharing a common concern with other groups in the community in the solution of problems facing the community. It is being forced to defend itself against the consequences of its own direct impact on the community and its environment. Its own conduct is at issue.

Thirdly, there is increasing recognition by management leaders and others of the need for governmental guidance and regulation. It is apparent that the public demands vigorous response with an intensity not previously experienced, that competitive factors may impede or retard the degree of business response, and that the problem has become too big for business to solve on its own. Thus President Nixon's then science adviser, Dr. Lee A. DuBridge in June [1970] described the role of government to be the imposition of regulations to protect responsible companies from the less enlightened. On the other hand, some are still calling for business mobilization on an industrywide basis for solution of environmental problems, in order to head off otherwise inevitable governmental action.

Thus, in the environmental areas, corporations are faced with a challenge which is clearly different from the questions presented in the traditional areas of social responsibility. In the environmental area, corporate management is not concerned with the role of business as an instrument of social progress or as a participant on a relatively limited level in programs for social or community improvement. The questions for discussion are not such items as whether corporate funds might more properly be expended for conventional philanthropic objectives by shareholders than by corporate managers, or whether banks and department stores are well advised to expend corporate funds to help sustain the inner cities to which their businesses are inextricably interrelated. The questions in the environmental field relate to harder decisions of more formidable import. In summary, management faces a crisis in which business is vulnerable because the problem is one which it has created itself, where the objective of the struggle is to anticipate or shape the pattern of inevitable legislation, where the stakes are so high that the motivation is essentially one of self-preservation, and in consequence, where the corporate response may no longer be fairly regarded as voluntary.

Because business response is no longer one that reflects relative freedom of choice, business has, for the first time in an area of corporate responsibility been obligated to make major expenditures. Pollution control costs have emerged as a substantial item in the capital budget, unlike other areas where corporate social efforts have never had any real impact on earnings per share. It has been estimated that industry is spending from $1.5 to $3 billion a year on air and water pollution abatement. For example, air and water pollution abatement equipment in the new Union Oil Company of California refinery near Chicago cost $37 million, or 18 percent, of the total cost of $200 million; Sun Oil Company similarly advises that environmental control equipment will account for at least 10 percent of the cost of its new Puerto Rico refinery. Bethlehem Steel Corporation reports that 11 percent of its capital budget is represented by pollution control facilities.

Union Carbide Corporation advises that with pollution abatement costs running at approximately 3 percent to 4 percent of its capital budget, increased operating costs—without regard to such items as the cost of servicing the increased debt involved in the increased capital cost, or the increased depreciation charges—were reducing net income after taxes by 8 cents per share and that this figure would increase at the rate of 2 cents per share per year.

For the foregoing reasons, the term—corporate social responsibility—hardly seems applicable to problems in the environmental field, whether or not it may have usefulness elsewhere. The battle which business must fight relates so much to the vitals of the enterprise that questions of "enlightened self interest" or concern with long range profit-making potential, or good public relations—the typical justifications for corporate social responsibility in the area of voluntary activity—are hardly appropriate to represent the hard decisions and substantial expenditures which business is being forced to make to satisfy the public demand for environmental protection.

These hard decisions must be considered against a changing corporate background. As the problems of American society have grown more complex, as concern with its fundamental values have become more widespread particularly among younger people, as the size and economic influence of the largest five hundred industrial corporations have increased to the point where in 1968 they represented almost 64 percent of total industrial sales and 74.4 percent of total profits. An increasing politicalization of the large public American corporation seems to be taking place. Such developments as Project GM, the Council for Economic Priorities, confrontations at the annual meetings of shareholders of American Telephone, Bank of America, Boeing

Aircraft, Chase Manhattan Bank, Dow Chemical, Gulf Oil, International Business Machines, Minneapolis Honeywell, Union Carbide, and others, the public concern of a company such as Polaroid, whether it should continue to do business in South Africa, the demand of the United Church of Christ that Gulf Oil terminate its concession in Angola, all illustrate this trend. It is marked in appeals to the corporation's shareholders—not as shareholders, but as persons whose fundamental interests as citizens transcend their relatively minor interests as shareholders—as well as appeals to consumers and the public. It is a war waged for control of public opinion. The annual shareholder meeting at this moment is merely the forum for attracting the public eye and ear.

However, it does not seem realistic to suppose that the process will stop there. The Securities and Exchange Commission is under increasing pressure to broaden the availability of the proxy solicitation machinery for utilization by "public interest" groups for these purposes and is presently reviewing its proxy solicitation rules. If SEC Rule 14a-8 is liberalized as seems likely, and the management proxy solicitation is required to include an extended range of proposals by shareholders, to allocate a reasonable amount of space to the reasons advanced for such proposals in place of the present indefensible one-hundred-word limitation, and perhaps to list shareholder nominees for the Board as recently proposed by Campaign GM, the corporate proxy solicitation process financed by corporate funds may well provide a forum for increased politicalization of the corporation, which may ultimately lead to significant changes in American corporate life. [See Section III of this volume, Campaign GM.] Already, it is apparent that nonprofit institutions, such as universities and churches, will provide a substantial base to mount such efforts. [The SEC rule was liberalized in September 1972.—Ed.]

Indeed, whether or not these efforts will be successful in the proxy contest itself is not critical. The critical element is that corporations will face increasing efforts in this area and that the public opinion mobilized and intensified by such efforts will likely force management to accept in substantial measure the objectives of such campaigns. Management may win all the proxy battles and still lose the war....

So much for the background. What are some of the hard questions presented for American corporations by environmental problems? Without in any way intending to present an all-inclusive list, some of the major issues would appear to include the following:

(a) Will competitive factors in the marketplace prevent individual businesses from dealing effectively with pollution factors inherent in their operations so long as pollution abatement is a matter in which management has some significant freedom of decision?

(b) To what extent can such competitive factors be reduced or eliminated as a result of the continuing intensification of public demand or through the voluntary establishment of industrywide standards by trade associations or similar organizations? Will any such collective efforts present problems under the antitrust laws?

(c) To what extent are industrywide governmental standards, controls, and enforcement necessary or desirable?

(d) To what extent are governmental financial incentives, such as tax credits, accelerated depreciation deductions, subsidies and the like, necessary or desirable? In other words, to what extent should taxpayers generally pay the bill?

(e) To what extent will the costs involved in pollution abatement, which are not borne by government and therefore by taxpayers, be borne by consumers through higher prices?

(f) To what extent will such costs be absorbed internally, affect previously accepted profit margins, reduce earnings, and therefore be borne by shareholders?

(g) Will environmental concern lead to governmental determination of social priorities? Will utility commissions, for example, be forced to choose between power and pollution? Will other agencies be forced to face similar decisions in other industries? In brief, will environmental concern lead to a degree of governmental economic planning, not previously seen in American life?

(h) Will environmental concern lead to a continuing politicalization of the American corporation through increased use of the existing proxy solicitation machinery by "public interest" groups, or through confrontations at shareholder meetings?

(i) Will environmental concern lead to fundamental changes in the proxy solicitation machinery itself through changes in SEC Rule 14a-8, or through such changes in organic corporation law as involved in Professor [David L.] Ratner's recent suggestion of the substitution of "one man, one vote" in place of "one share, one vote," or in the proposal for the addition of "consumer," "supplier," and "dealer" directors to the General Motors Board contained in the Campaign GM Round II Proxy Statement?

TACTICS OF PUBLIC-INTEREST GROUPS [4]

Public-interest groups are pressing a record number of proposals for corporate action at . . . annual stockholder meetings. . . . But at the same time the corporate social-responsibility movement is broadening its tactics.

As specialized public-interest groups proliferate, coalesce and sometimes bicker, corporate challenges are increasingly taking a legalistic turn. Lawsuits are being filed. Petitions are being made to government agencies that regulate corporations and industries.

. . . [In March 1973] for example, a Federal district court held the directors and officers of the New York Telephone Company personally liable for a $50,000 contribution from

[4] From "Corporate-Responsibility Groups Broaden Tactics," by Marylin Bender, staff reporter. New York *Times*. p 55-6. Ap. 2, '73. © 1973 by the New York Times Company. Reprinted by permission.

corporate funds to a state bond issue referendum in violation of the state election law.

The suit against the company had originally been filed by the Project on Corporate Responsibility, a Washington-based organization that conducted Campaign GM in 1970 and 1971.

Though that proxy contest against the auto maker stimulated the interest of college students and institutional investors on their shareholder-voting duties, none of its proposals received more than 2 percent of total vote.

"The near impossibility of actually winning a shareholder campaign coupled with the complexity of filing an acceptable proposal have convinced many groups that other tactics may be more effective," notes the Council on Economic Priorities in its forthcoming report on the corporate-responsibility movement.

CEP, a nonprofit, New York-based research group, has itself joined with others in a case involving advertising claims made by Standard Oil of California for its F310 gasoline additive.

Ironically, the Project on Corporate Responsibility may resort to legal action to save its own life.

For the last two and a half years, the Washington-based organization of lawyers and researchers has been seeking tax-exempt status as a public-interest law firm and research center. Currently, some $500,000 in foundation grants are tied up pending approval by the United States Treasury for such tax exemption.

. . . [In March 1973], Philip C. Sorensen, chairman and a founder of the organization, said he had been advised by his attorney to expect a negative ruling soon from the chief counsel of the Internal Revenue Service despite earlier indications of approval from the staff of the IRS exempt-organization bureau. The IRS confers such exemptions if it views a public-interest law firm as engaging in educational or charitable activities.

Asserting that "these actions indicate political interference," Mr. Sorensen said that if the tax exemption is denied, "we would go to Federal court and seek some sort of injunctive relief to permit us to survive while the issue of the tax exemption was litigated. Otherwise, the whole question becomes moot. With these grants outstanding, they can delay us right out of existence."

Application Amended

He pointed out that last June, the tax-exemption application was amended to sever the Project's shareholder proxy activities from its litigation and research because word had been received "that the IRS says proxy fights are not tax exempt."

A spokesman for the Internal Revenue Service, declining comment on the status of the application said last week that there had been no published ruling on the tax-exempt standing of proxy challenges but that applications for tax-exempt status are subject to varying degrees of interpretation and scrutiny.

Mr. Sorensen and his associates argue that proxy fights like Campaign GM are educational. However, they did reorganize their activities.

In the reorganization, the original name—Project on Corporate Responsibility—was assigned to proxy challenges, and the Center on Corporate Responsibility was set up to pursue research and shareholder litigation. The Project has submitted three proposals to seven corporations for this year's annual meetings.

The International Business Machines Corporation, Levi Strauss & Co. and the Xerox Corporation are being asked to establish procedures for shareholder nominations to the boards of directors that would appear on the corporate proxies.

Two other proposals on political influence were directed at the Eastman Kodak Company, the General Motors Corporation, the Union Oil Company and the International Telephone and Telegraph Company. One proposal would require disclosures about political contributions. The other, aimed at corporate lobbying efforts, asks the companies to describe how they communicated their positions "concerning any matter of unusual significance to the corporation" to the Federal Government as well as the names of corporate and Government officials involved in its news release. The project linked the proposal "to the ITT affair as an example of the kind of 'impropriety' and damage to the corporation's reputation the disclosures called for in this proposal can prevent."

Although the proposals will not appear on any of the corporate proxy statements (except possibly General Motors, which is still being processed) because the Securities and Exchange Commission ruled them ineligible on a technical point, they will be submitted from the floor at the annual meetings.

As the CEP report comments, "Many groups raising them [proxy proposals] feel the first step to reform is forcing investors to consider them."

All told, some twenty groups are submitting at least three dozen proposals to as many major corporations this year. They confront operations in Southern Africa, military contracts and conversion to peacetime production, the environment, consumerism, minority employment, political influence and reform of the corporate structure.

Nearly half of the proposals emanate from church groups who seem to be carrying the ball on the Southern Africa and military-industrial issues. A coalition of churches has asked for disclosure of operations in Southern Africa from eight corporations.

Resolutions Withdrawn

Several of them—the Burroughs Corporation, ITT, Texaco, Xerox and . . . Ford—subsequently agreed to supply the information, and the resolutions were withdrawn.

The proposal drew only 1.03 percent of the vote at the First National City Bank meeting last week, well below the

SEC's 3 percent requirement for submission again within five years.

The church-sponsored resolution on Exxon relates to exploration for oil off the shore of the Portuguese territory of Angola. Exxon has applied for an exploration license. The churches want a broad-based committee to study the implications of this venture and to report on it.

Continental Oil and Phillips Petroleum are being asked to wind up operations in Namibia (another group of Episcopal churchmen are asking the same of American Metal Climax and Newmont Mining) while Mobil Oil and Newmont have been requested to initiate equality of job opportunity in their operations in countries that practice racial discrimination.

Clergy and Laity Concerned, an antiwar group, have filed resolutions with Honeywell, General Electric and Exxon asking these corporations to stop producing antipersonnel weapons, to suspend military contracts with Government agencies related to the war in Southeast Asia and to establish committees to study conversion to civilian-oriented production. . . .

The CEP report observes that "with expansion and diversification and the definition of broad common areas of interest also comes discord and disagreement." Allusion is made to the contradictory resolutions from two church groups within the Protestant coalition filed with one company, Newmont Mining, one urging the company to leave Namibia, the other to practice equal job opportunity there.

Competition Exists

There has also been both cooperation and competition between the research groups established to help institutional investors make up their minds on voting their proxies.

The Investor Responsibility Research Center, Inc., established in Washington . . . [in 1972] and funded by the Ford and Rockefeller Foundations and the Carnegie Corporation has enrolled fifty-two subscribers, the majority of them universities and foundations, and has thus far given them detailed analyses of half a dozen proposals.

Partly because of the existence of the IRRC, interest in the second institutional-investors conference planned for this month by the Center on Corporate Responsibility was so slight that it was canceled.

"One of the basic things we're after are more fundamental questions than appear on the resolutions," Mr. Sorensen said. "We're disappointed if institutions think everything's resolved by subscribing to the Investor Research group. These are the surface issues."

The Center on Corporate Responsibility is undertaking extensive research projects on such topics as corporations whose business is based primarily on women and the plight of hotel employees. The aims of the research program, says Susan Gross, director of research and education, "is to produce exposés to pressure corporations to change policies" and to inform other advocacy groups such as black or feminist organizations "of the need to focus more on corporations."

The chief difference between the Center and the loosely constructed Nader movement is the former's single-minded emphasis on corporations where some of the Nader groups and other public-interest law firms and research organizations are looking toward government agencies and other aspects of consumer issues.

"Crowding" Is Cited

"The field is getting a little bit crowded but so far not overcrowded," said John Simon, a Yale law professor and coauthor of *The Ethical Investor*, a study of the problems universities face in making social decisions about their investment portfolios.

Professor Simon is also chairman of Yale University's Advisory Committee on Investor Responsibility, appointed . . . [in 1972] to make recommendations on how the university should vote its proxies. An open meeting . . . called by the committee drew an audience of ten, half of them committee members. Similar signs of massive indifference were noticed at a hearing by Harvard's committee for the same purpose. . . . [In 1972] black students staged a sit-in at Harvard asking the university to sell its stock in Gulf Oil, which operates in Angola.

Nevertheless, Professor Simon does not believe that corporate responsibility is withering away. "Corporate gadflies will keep it alive even if students aren't beating up the flames so institutions will have to deal with it," he said.

. . . [In March 1973] Exxon sent several representatives to tell institutional investors at a forum sponsored by the Africa Policy Information Institute why they should vote no on the church-sponsored resolution on Exxon's exploration of Angola.

The Exxon people stressed their belief that the primary corporate mission was to develop energy resources. But they said that international and domestic public opinion were also a genuine concern, and that if public opinion and Government policy were ever jelled in opposition to Exxon's activity in Southern Africa, it might be dropped.

THE LEGAL EXPLOSION [5]

There was a time, and it was not so very long ago, when the legal departments of many sizable corporations led relatively low-pressure lives. The chores they handled were remote from the major decisions of policy, and the legal staff was, accordingly, somewhat remote from the chief executives. That was, of course, before the great legal explosion—before class-action suits became a kind of popular sport, before consumerism, environmentalism, and other forms of Naderism, before Americans in general became so litigious. Since the great explosion began, the top executives have had some trouble escaping from legal matters—not to mention

[5] From "The 'Legal Explosion' Has Left Business Shell-Shocked," by Eleanore Carruth, associate editor. Fortune. 87:65-9+. Ap. '73. Reprinted by permission of Fortune magazine; © 1973 Time Inc.

their own lawyers. Speaking of his company's general counsel recently, chairman [now retired] Richard Gerstenberg of General Motors said, "Mr. [Ross] Malone and I go pretty steady."

Businessmen have always been pretty good at griping about laws and regulations, especially since the New Deal. But the tenor of their remarks has clearly shifted in the past half dozen years or so. The New Deal imposed a new array of burdens on corporations; the recent legal explosion has created some potential liabilities that threaten their survival. "Corporations in the early thirties may have felt they were living through the French and Russian revolutions combined," says Joseph Weiner, a New York University law professor and consultant, "but that wasn't a patch on what is going on now." William May, chairman of American Can, put the case more starkly: "We are fighting for our lives."

In addition to creating some enormous new liabilities, the legal explosion has left corporations exposed to numerous bouts of litigation. . . . Over the past six years there has been almost a 100 percent increase in lawsuits brought before the Federal courts in six major areas where corporations are heavily involved in litigation. But the cases that get to court are the least of the matter. The business of lawyers, after all, is to avoid litigation, to head off showdowns—by dealing more effectively with regulatory agencies, bending corporate behavior into line with new rules and standards, negotiating out-of-court settlements, and the like. This practice of "preventive law" appears to have grown about as fast as litigation. In addition, more and more corporations have decided that they must participate more strenuously in the framing of legislation and regulation.

It's a Growth Industry

In an effort to gauge the impact of the legal explosion, *Fortune* has surveyed a cross section of top US corporations, by size and type of business. They were asked about the growth of their legal departments and legal costs; they were also asked a variety of questions about the problems besetting them now and the extent to which these have been changing. Sixty-five companies replied.

The survey data suggest that the annual bill for legal departments and outside counsel (excluding overseas operations) is something on the order of $1.3 billion for the 1,300 US companies listed in *Fortune*'s annual directories (i.e., the 500 largest industrials, the Second 500, and the 50 largest commercial banks, life-insurance companies, diversified financial companies, retailers, transportation companies, and utilities). The bill for all US corporations may well amount to something on the order of $3 billion. The companies reporting to *Fortune* had increased their own legal outlays by 75 percent in the past half dozen years, one and a half times as fast as in the previous half dozen. The number of lawyers employed in the legal departments of the reporting companies has increased by a third since 1966; the rise in 1960-66 was about 25 percent.

How Mr. May Spends His Time

But even these figures only partly suggest the new legal pressures on corporations. The legal wars have become too important for corporations to leave to their lawyers, and so a lot of top-executive time is given over to fighting them. "I probably spend about 60 percent of my time on legal problems," says American Can's May, "more than twice as much as five years ago." May's figure does not include much time spent on actual litigation—once it gets to that, lawyers take over—but the hours spent on "paralegal" matters, i.e., planning corporate behavior in response to new or proposed regulations as well as court decisions that change the rules. The direct financial stake in many current lawsuits and regulatory brawls is staggering, but the indirect stakes are even more immense. Indeed, they concern the corporation's basic competitive posture. In many areas, for example, compliance with the letter and spirit of the law entails heavy

Pressure on American Standard

On balance, the pressures to settle class actions are great. If the corporations lose, a court may award higher damages than they could have bargained for. Furthermore, the very fact of being assailed as a polluter, or price fixer, or discriminator can damage a company's reputation. The prospective damage to its public image was a factor in American Standard's decision . . . [in 1970] to pay $15 million in settlement of four antitrust class actions.

There are now pending in the Federal district courts at least one thousand class-action suits involving corporations, and the totals are still growing. Moreover, a number of states have enacted statutes similar to the Federal rule, and some of them have gone even further. California, for instance, sets no minimum requirement for damages in consumer class actions, whereas Federal courts usually require each individual plaintiff to be able to claim injury amounting to at least $10,000.

Now a move is afoot in Congress to permit individuals to aggregate claims. That would open up the possibility of broad attacks by consumers, and corporations eyeing the proposed legislation are naturally somewhat upset by it. Says a lawyer who is helping to frame the legislation:

These people are really scared. The ironic thing is that most consumers are still completely unaware of the possibilities for class action. One can only wonder what the situation will be when all the groups that can stand to benefit have marshaled their attack.

In some areas of the law, meanwhile, public agencies are encouraging prospective plaintiffs to marshal those attacks. The Equal Employment Opportunity Commission, for instance, is encouraging private suits against alleged discriminators; and other Federal agencies, including the Federal Trade Commission and the Environmental Protection Agency, are seeking new laws under which individuals can bring their own class-action suits. Two out of three corporations in the *Fortune* survey say they are now either defendants in, or threatened by, class-action suits. The American College of Trial Lawyers is leading a counterattack to reform the reformed rules and make it more difficult to bring class suits.

Where the Trouble Comes From

Even aside from its role in encouraging class actions, the Federal Government has been a major source of the corporations' new legal miseries. When *Fortune* asked those in its survey to rank the principal generators of their legal problems, forty-four out of the sixty-five responding companies ranked the Federal government first, and all but one assigned it some role. Second place in this ranking was won by "state and local governments." But the private sector itself did not do badly: ten companies ranked it first and twenty-five had it second. Within the private sector, the principal sources of legal problems were (in order) "individuals other than stockholders," other corporations, private organizations, and stockholders.

Fortune also asked the corporations to consider eight broad areas of the law, and to rank them according to the amount of the legal department's time that each one was taking up these days. The areas: antitrust, securities and stockholder matters, consumerism, environment, fair-employment practices, safety, government contracts, and wage-price controls, along with "other." The answers suggest that legal problems are remarkably diversified: one third of the companies actually ranked "other" first, and no single source of trouble dominated the returns.

The survey then asked for rankings based on the degree of *concern* each area represented for the future of the corporation. On this ranking, the handling of contracts and of wage-price controls, which had done fairly well as consumers of legal-department time, fell to the bottom; but among the remaining entries there still were no standouts. These rankings are clearly different from what would have turned up in any such exercise a decade ago. "Ten years ago, we would have said our worries were 'antitrust and then everything else lumped together,'" remarks one executive interviewed by *Fortune*. "Not anymore." Says F. Mark Garlinghouse, the general counsel for American Telephone & Telegraph, "Our No. 1 problem changes from month to month." On balance, it seems clear that five areas—antitrust, securities and stock-holder matters, consumerism, environment, and fair-employment practices—are matters of serious and widespread concern.

New Dimensions in Antitrust

Antitrust still weighs pretty heavily on business. About a quarter of those in the survey gave it top billing both as a time consumer and as a source of corporate concern. The rise of class actions has given an interesting new dimension to antitrust law. Antitrust, indeed, has been the battleground on which *most* of the large class-action settlements have been won so far, and it accounts for three hundred of the thousand-odd class-action cases pending in Federal courts. Under Federal law, only in antitrust cases can plaintiffs (other than the US Government) sue for triple the amount of actual damage; and there is no minimum requirement for damage in antitrust matters. As if that weren't enough, there are antitrust statutes now in some forty states, many of which have full-time staffs filing more suits and bolder ones.

Of greater importance to business has been a constant pushing at the boundaries of antitrust law in recent years. The Federal Trade Commission is ambitiously sizing up market concentrations in whole industries and alleging that certain practices are unfair—even when there is no contention that they are collusive. Last year, for example, it brought a pioneering complaint against the four largest cereal manufacturers, charging them with a "shared monopoly" simply because together they controlled 90 percent of the market.

Lawsuits in the Club

Another arresting new phenomenon is the growing number of suits pitting corporations against one another under the antitrust laws. The number of private antitrust suits filed annually was running at about 255 until 1960 but has been climbing steadily since; . . . [in 1972] 1,299 private antitrust suits were brought in the Federal courts. ("Private" also includes state and local governments.) Most of these, of course, involved corporations as either defendants or plaintiffs, and more and more of these battles are between giants: Control Data versus IBM, Xerox versus IBM, Litton versus Xerox, ITT versus General Telephone. This kind of thing didn't happen ten years ago. "It just wasn't done," remarks one Justice Department official. "It would have been like suing a member of your own club."

To some extent, the corporate warfare may simply reflect the increase in new technologies—control of which is inevitably a matter of dispute. But some lawyers also say corporations that couldn't succeed in the marketplace are trying to win their fortunes in court.

Corporations are shouldering new burdens in another area that has long been regulated, their relationships with shareholders and investors in general. Indeed, these matters come closest to being a universal headache: 85 percent of the companies in the *Fortune* survey gave securities matters *some* ranking as consumers of legal time, and one in ten cited them as No. 1. They rank lower on the scale of concern than of time, but even here they are higher than they were in the past—and with good reason.

The number of suits filed in securities matters has trebled in the last half dozen years, and in several significant suits the courts have become much more strict and specific in their interpretations of the basic New Deal statutes. Their rulings have greatly increased the standard of care— and work—required. "Ten years ago," says a lawyer who specializes in securities law, "what a company said in its annual report was pretty much up to the public-relations department. Today, what you say or fail to say, even in a press release, can be the basis for some monster lawsuit."

Concern About the Consumers

Consumerism (with the term defined to include product safety) takes up somewhat less legal-department time than do securities matters. But it now rivals antitrust in the concern it generates. Small wonder. In the last six years Congress has passed more than a dozen pieces of major consumer legislation on matters ranging from package labeling to truth-in-lending. Additional measures were introduced in the last Congress, including some sweeping legislation that would set up a consumer-protection agency, would broaden even further the powers of the FTC, and would provide for consumer class actions. So far, not many consumer suits have been brought in the Federal courts, because Federal law has very few provisions that entitle ordinary citizens to sue. But the Government itself has many different ways of acting for them; by one recent count, there are twenty Federal agencies concerned with consumer affairs, and they are spewing out more and stricter regulations all the time.

The FTC, which already has very broad powers over consumer matters, is particularly exercised these days about advertising and labeling. The commission now requires corporations to supply on demand full documentation for their advertising claims. To comply with this directive, one big manufacturer of consumer goods spends $500,000 annually, more than double the amount it would have had to spend before the new rule.

The $90 Million Wheels

Quite apart from Federal law, there has been an enormous and simultaneous growth in state and local legislation. It has resulted in the establishment of offices and bureaus concerned with consumer affairs in forty state governments and in many more counties and cities. On these lower levels there is more leeway for class suits; some notion of what is at stake in those proposed laws to broaden the base for class-action suits can be discerned in that most activist state of California. Two truck owners there are suing General Motors on behalf of 200,000 others, demanding free replacement of allegedly defective wheels, at an estimated cost to GM of some $90 million.

Legal problems associated with environmental issues are by no means as universal a worry as consumerism; nevertheless, they represent serious new concerns, particularly to manufacturing and public-utilities companies. One tenth of those in *Fortune*'s survey ranked environment as their major legal concern in the future, and another tenth placed it second. In addition to stimulating new enforcement of an 1899 act, the public demands for a better environment have prompted Congress to enact half a dozen major new laws since 1965, constructing a tight regulatory system for air, water, and noise pollution. The Environmental Protection Agency, set up late in 1970, and other agencies have barraged corporations with new standards to meet and procedures to follow.

The courts have affirmed the right, under these laws, of environmentalists to sue corporations in the "public interest" (as opposed to private, pecuniary interest). Recent amendments to the Federal Water Pollution Control and Clean Air acts specifically provide for citizens' suits. Back in 1966, the number of environmental suits filed by the government in Federal courts was minuscule; by . . . [1972] the number was over 250. In 1969, the year environmental litigation began to catch fire at the state level, more than 750 court actions were brought under state laws; both legislation and litigation have been proliferating since then.

Drowning in the Law

Consider the consequent plight of, for instance, Con Edison, which is "engulfed in a tidal wave of legalism," as chairman Charles Luce puts it. Almost the least of the matter is the $193 million the company paid out last year for environmental protection—the extra cost of low-sulphur fuel, underground transmission lines, plant redesign and conversion. Con Edison is also defending legal actions brought by citizens' groups protesting plans for all seven of its proposed new generating sites. "We naturally try to head off legal problems, but it's no easy task," says Luce. "After we've finally convinced the people living next door to a proposed plant that it really won't harm them, we find ourselves locked in conflict with, say, the fishermen, who wish we'd just go find ourselves another river."

On the other hand, Con Ed can't just sit still. The company must continue to select sites as best it can and go ahead with orders and construction, placing its bets on what the courts will decide. 'It's conceivable that we may find ourselves with a half-billion dollars' worth of equipment that we can't use," says Luce. "It is the kind of thing you pray over."

The corporations in *Fortune*'s survey placed the legal problems associated with fair-employment practices lower on their scale of urgency, but several chief executives indicated that this area may be just heating up. It was only . . . [in 1972] that the Equal Employment Opportunity Commission, the agency that monitors Title VII of the Civil Rights Act, got the right to bring its own suits. . . . In addition, with a backlog of some 55,000 complaints, the commission has stated that it aims to promote private action by employees, and so it has established a Litigation Services Branch. More than one thousand fair-employment suits were filed in the Federal courts last year, many by individuals suing on behalf of a class. Corporations are liable to back-pay penalties in fair-employment-practice suits, and American Telephone & Telegraph early . . . [in 1973] agreed to provide some $15 million in back pay in settlement of one suit.

Work for 40,000 Lawyers

It comes as no surprise, all things considered, that corporations are racking up some hefty legal bills these days. Legal expenditures for corporations in the *Fortune* survey averaged about $1.5 million per company. The figure excludes outlays for overseas operations, which also appear to be mounting rapidly, for work done on patent problems, or for liability-insurance premiums.

Fortune's figure of $3 billion for total business legal costs is obviously a "ball-park" estimate. It is known, however, that US corporations now employ 40,000 or so lawyers, and their cost, combined with that of supporting personnel, appears to be on the order of $2 billion. The companies in the survey indicated that they spent somewhat less for outside counsel than for their own legal departments.

However, it is clear from the survey that corporations vary considerably in the amounts of money spent on legal matters. Nine of the surveyed companies disbursed about half the total legal dollars, and one industrial giant alone spent $10 million.

The general trend of legal expenses, however, is unmistakable. The figures suggest an average annual growth rate of about 10 percent during the past six years. Only three companies reported lower outlays in 1972 than in 1966, and 35 percent had more than doubled their outlays. Some reported that their legal expenses had risen over 500 percent in the past twelve years.

Many corporations have acquired legal staffs of substantial size only in recent years, and the rise of these inside departments accounts for some of the big jumps. In 1960, more than half the companies in the survey had no more than four lawyers in residence; now less than a fourth have so few. There has been some net increase in the number of small staffs—five to ten lawyers—and a more rapid increase of medium-sized to large departments. Six companies reported that they now employ fifty or more lawyers in their legal departments (the largest, General Electric, had 150);

only two were that big in 1960. The median staff had doubled (to eight lawyers) over the decade; so had the number of lawyers per company (to twenty).

A Case for Inside Counsel

Most chief executives of corporations with substantial legal departments look at legal expenses as an overhead cost that shouldn't ordinarily go up as rapidly as business volume. The legal liabilities are rising rapidly too, of course; still, top management at many companies believes that the time has come to hold down on those cost increases. A number of executives interviewed said that they were working their legal staffs harder or giving more legal chores to non-lawyers (who cost a lot less); a few also admitted cutting corners on the quality of some legal work.

Since company lawyers come cheaper than outside counsel, substantial savings can often be achieved by handling more of the legal business in-house. The legal department is taking on more of the routine work—e.g., handling contracts and filings with regulatory agencies—and is increasingly involved in more sophisticated problems too. Many chief executives told *Fortune* that legal costs would now be completely out of hand if they had not beefed up their own departments in recent years. One large corporation estimates that it costs only $15 an hour for the inside staff to handle run-of-the-mine matters that an outside law firm might bill at $50.

Not that in-house operations come cheap these days. Ten companies in the survey maintain legal staffs costing over $1 million annually—$10 million was the top budget—and eleven others spend more than $500,000 apiece.

It's Expensive in New York

But the cost of outside counsel has been rising even faster. Law firms have increased their fees substantially in the last several years. Hourly rates for standard legal work in New York, an expensive legal town, . . . jumped from

$40 at the top corporate law firms in 1965 to $80 . . . [in
1973]—and on complex problems, requiring a lot of senior
partners' time, the hourly rate is a lot higher.

Corporate executives still turn naturally to their outside
counsel when they're dealing with issues that are especially
sensitive (e.g., mergers and acquisitions) or new and un-
charted (e.g., fair-employment practices and the environment). And corporate managers and directors seem more
and more to want an outside opinion simply to minimize
their own risk in dealing with a weighty matter. "It's sort
of like sprinkling holy water on the situation," is the way
one chief executive puts it.

And, of course, corporations usually go outside for counsel when they get into real litigation. "That's when the
meter really runs," says an executive whose company is a
defendant in several major lawsuits. The meter registered
$15 million for legal fees and expenses paid to Control
Data by IBM as part of the $60 million cash settlement of
an antitrust case. IBM's own legal bill during the battle is
believed to have exceeded $60 million.

Thirteen companies in *Fortune*'s survey reported that
they had spent more than $1 million apiece on outside
counsel in 1972; only one had spent that much in 1960.
Almost a third of the companies had each engaged fifty or
more outside law firms . . . , more than twice as many as in
1960. The typical company had increased the number of
outside counsel it used to twenty firms, from fourteen a
dozen years ago. (The number of outside firms employed
depends on many things—for example, on how many states
and localities the company operates in.)

The Ins Versus the Outs

Relations between inside and outside counsel are usually amicable, sometimes warm, almost always businesslike
—but scarcely ever without an undercurrent of competition. Outside law firms can offer a corporate client the
special expertise that comes from their wide-ranging ex-

perience and special resources. They can also fairly point out that the advice they give is somewhat more objective than the advice an employee can give his boss. "We don't have to tack," is the way a nautically minded senior partner of one blue-ribbon firm says it. "You can't give independent advice to the chief executive who controls your destiny."

The in-house lawyers, on the other hand, can argue that they have a greater depth of understanding, based on a more intimate knowledge of their companies. "It's just too expensive to be repeatedly involved in educating outside counsel," says Robert Estes, the senior vice president who heads General Electric's legal department. Some in-house counsel suggest that outside firms have an incentive to run the meter.

The highest and perhaps most difficult duty of any in-house lawyer is to advise the chief executive in all the legal "gray areas" that contain potential threats to the corporation. "That's what lawyers are for," says Carl Desch, senior vice president of First National City Bank. But such judgments are increasingly difficult to make, because there are more problems, more untested areas, and "you have to guess at what the courts will do," in the words of one chief executive. "I find myself constantly thinking about what the law will become, how a judge will rule tomorrow," says Pierce McCreary, general counsel for Kennecott Copper.

McCreary happens to have an interesting "gray-area problem" right now. The FTC is challenging Kennecott's acquisition of Peabody Coal on grounds not previously invoked: that the merger will probably lead to concentration in the coal industry. In these gray areas—where counsel cannot say for sure what the law will or will not permit—he has to appraise the risks of "catching" a suit and also the chances of winning it.

Given the nature of the current problems, it is not surprising that more and more chief executives tend to be lawyers themselves. More than 20 percent of those who head companies on *Fortune*'s five hundred and "fifty largest" lists are lawyers by training; this figure is up from less than 15 percent back in 1959.

But many chief executives nevertheless make the point that, when big decisions have to be made, there are distinct limits to the value of legal opinions. "Counsel are invaluable in calculating the legal risks," one chief executive observed recently, "but we have to work out the risk-reward ratios." Chairman C. Peter McColough of Xerox, himself a lawyer, says, "I don't want the lawyers to put themselves in my shoes. They give me a legal opinion, but I have a lot of other factors to consider."

There are times when the chief executives must choose between inside and outside legal counsel, whose opinions sometimes differ; there are times, indeed, when the boss must overrule them both. RCA Chairman Robert Sarnoff has observed that it's easy to stay out of trouble by letting your lawyers keep you cautious. "But it's also an easy way to go nowhere. It is extremely important to be sure the legal department doesn't inhibit imaginative business thinking and innovation."

An Ounce of Prevention

The practice of "preventive law" is a major new part of the management process at many corporations. Preventive law may mean, for example, requiring clearance of major press releases, holding classes on antitrust for middle management, even setting up whole new departments to handle consumer and environmental affairs. At B. F. Goodrich it means periodic employee-attitude surveys designed, among other things, to head off trouble about fair-employment practices.

"It's all useful but all limited," says legal consultant Weiner. "You never fully succeed, and it is next to impossible to anticipate all the areas in which you may be hit." As a practical matter, says TWA's chairman Charles Tillinghast Jr., "the volume of laws and regulations is such that no one can comply faithfully with all the rules. No large organization can effectively police all its employees."

The truth of that observation was demonstrated early this year, when the Environmental Protection Agency slapped a $7 million fine on Ford Motor Company. Employees at its testing center had modified engines to meet emission standards. The company itself caught and reported the tampering, but Administrator William Ruckelshaus declared that EPA nevertheless would not "condone unlawful practices by responsible employees at the operating level of the corporation."

And so, in an effort to minimize the threat posed by law, corporations are increasingly active in fighting proposed legislation. "We have to worry about three thousand bills that are introduced, not just the three hundred-odd that are passed," says First National City's Desch. American Can's chairman, William May, observed recently, "Once the law is on the books, you have usually lost the battle." Many corporations have greatly expanded their Washington legal staffs and have their top executives repeatedly hustling to Capitol Hill to testify on all sorts of bills and regulations. Says Arthur Wood, board chairman of Sears, Roebuck, "You just have to work with legislative committees on the facts and what kind of regulations are compatible with the consumers' interest and the business interest."

Whether this kind of effort to reconcile the two will pay off is anybody's guess right now. But it seems reasonable to hope that some sense of common purpose can eventually be brought to the legal environment, and that "this whole adversary thrust," as May has referred to it, can be deflected. A society in which business is endlessly besieged by legal problems cannot be very healthy for very long.

CORPORATE RESPONSIBILITY IN BRITAIN [6]

A [British government] White Paper issued on July 25 [1973] contains proposals for fundamental changes in the English company law. The main theme is to implement the concept that corporations have social responsibilities to employees and the public at large that temper the basic profit-making purpose.

A number of specific proposals are designed to assure corporate integrity and full disclosure so as to maintain public confidence in the free enterprise system.

Social Responsibilities

The White Paper accepts the basic profit-making purpose of corporations. It reaffirms the social desirability of the free enterprise system which enables capital to be accumulated and invested in risk-taking corporations, which create economic expansion, provide jobs and produce goods and services. However, it points out that a corporation must behave as a responsible part of society and the directors must reconcile the main profitability objective with responsibility to employees and the public.

The White Paper notes that in addition to specific proscriptions against such public matters as fraud, monopolization and pollution and regulation of such internal matters as severance pay and financial reporting, corporations have a more general and moral kind of social responsibility which is difficult to define and cannot be translated into specific laws. Several suggestions are put forward.

A Code of Conduct with some external sanction is suggested. . . . To protect directors against possible shareholder claims, it is suggested that corporations add to their charters a provision allowing directors to take social responsibility into account when exercising business judgment.

[6] From "Reform of English Company Law," by Martin Lipton, adjunct professor of law at New York University School of Law and member of a New York City law firm. *New York Law Journal.* p 1+. Ag. 9, '73. Reprinted by permission.

In addition it is suggested that corporations be required to include in their annual reports information on specific aspects of their response to the social environment. Disclosure is viewed as a major part of the enforcement of corporate social responsibility.

The details of increased employee participation in corporate affairs is left to a separate recommendation to be published later. . . . The trend is clearly in the direction of greater employee participation.

The role of the employees in the conduct of the company's affairs is a matter to which the government attach the greatest importance and which they have under urgent examination [the paper states]. The government believe that it is in the interests of all concerned, including those who provide the capital, that the employees should have an appropriate opportunity of influencing decisions which can closely affect their own interest.

Shareholder Responsibility. The White Paper rejects the two-tier board of directors (a supervisory board representing the shareholders over a management board) in use on the continent as being more suited to the continental pattern of large public companies being closely tied to financial institutions, than the English public ownership pattern which is similar to that in the United States. The White Paper notes the role of the outside director and it is indicated that consideration is being given to requiring that all public corporations have outside directors on their boards.

Institutional Investors. The concentration of institutional ownership of the larger public companies in England has been parallel to the experience in the United States. The White Paper notes the situation but does not propose any special responsibilities for institutional investors in relationship to their portfolio companies. There is a suggestion that responsibility to deal with mismanagement or poor management, rather than merely sell out, should be an obligation of institutional investors.

Disclosure. The White Paper embraces disclosure as an

essential part of the working of a free and fair economic
system:

> Obviously there are limits—imposed, for example, by the need
> to preserve commercial confidentiality in a competitive situation.
> But the bias must always be towards disclosure, with the burden
> of proof thrown on those who defend secrecy. The more people
> can see what is actually happening, the less likely they are to har-
> bour general suspicions—and the less opportunity there is for con-
> cealing improper or even criminal activities. Openness in com-
> pany affairs is the first principle in securing responsible behaviour.

The directors' report to the shareholders, the English
equivalent of our annual report, is to be expanded. The
White Paper sets forth a number of specific proposals.

> As possible examples of further disclosure in the directors' report,
> the directors may be required to report on the performance of
> their company in regard to the safety and health of the company's
> employees, on the number of consumer complaints and how they
> were dealt with and on the conduct of industrial relations. . . .
> The directors will be required to include in their report certain
> particulars of their own contracts of service; of their other inter-
> ests; of any dealings they have in the company's shares; and of
> transactions by the company and other companies in which they
> have any significant interest. . . .
> It may also be desirable to require the directors to disclose,
> more fully than is now the case, details of significant material
> acquisitions, realizations and contracts since the previous year.

The NYSE [New York Stock Exchange] is presently considering similar proposals in a soon-to-be-issued White Paper.

Inside Information. The White Paper shows that England is having the same problems of insider trading abuses
that we are having. The present method of dealing with
insider trading, through the rules of the stock exchange, and
in tender offers, the takeover panel, is to be supplemented
by both civil and criminal liability. The proposal treats non-
public market information—such as an intended takeover
bid—the same as inside corporate information. This issue is
still unsettled in the United States, with the SEC [Securities
and Exchange Commission] presently seeking comment and
preparing rule proposals.

The White Paper describes the underlying principles of the legislation as follows:

> The object of legislation on insider dealing must be to ensure that anyone who is in possession of information which would be likely, if generally known, to have a material effect on the price of the relevant securities refrains from dealing until the material has properly been made generally available. . . . [D]ealing in a company's securities by anyone who, by reason of his relationship with the company or with its officers, has information which he knows to be price sensitive, should be a criminal offence unless he can show that his primary intention in dealing at that particular time was not to make a profit or avoid a loss.

The present fourteen-day period for directors to report transactions in their companies' shares is to be shortened to the "shortest practicable period" and the stock exchange will make immediate public disclosure of the reports. . . .

Multinationals. Multinational companies operating in England are to be made subject to substantially the same disclosure requirements applicable to English companies.

Directors' Fiduciary Duties and Qualifications. The White Paper proposes a statutory restatement of a director's fiduciary duty to his corporation. In addition, to meet the conflict-of-interest problem, it is proposed that insider transactions be divided into those that can be dealt with through full disclosure and shareholder approval and those which are absolutely proscribed.

The Companies Act of 1948 empowers the court to disqualify a person for up to five years from being a director, or concerned in the management, of any company, if he is convicted of any criminal offense connected with promotion, management or liquidation of a company. The White Paper proposes to broaden director disqualification to conviction of any offense involving fraud or dishonesty whether or not in connection with a company, persistent default in complying with the Companies Act, or improper or reckless action in connection with the affairs of a company. Disqualification for incompetence was rejected on the ground that it cannot be easily defined in law or readily determined by a court.

Other Matters. The White Paper covers a number of other proposals and matters under consideration. Timely reporting is to be enforced strongly. Minority shareholder actions are to be made more widely available. Under consideration is a suggestion to distinguish more clearly between private and public corporations with only the latter subject to the full disclosure requirements. Public corporations would have to have minimum paid-up capital of $25,000 and there would be a new "small man" form of incorporation stopping short of limited liability.

Also under consideration are whether to liberalize the existing restrictions on a corporation lending money for the purchase of its shares and prohibiting limited voting or nonvoting shares.

III. CAMPAIGN GM

EDITOR'S INTRODUCTION

Campaign GM was the most publicized challenge to a corporation's authority in recent years. It pitted a leader of American capitalism against the nation's leading consumer advocate. This section begins with comments by James M. Roche (then chairman of General Motors) on the threat to free enterprise posed by adversaries who "crusade for radical changes in our system of corporate ownership." A statement by Ralph Nader follows, outlining what he had hoped to achieve at the General Motors shareholders' meeting. Next, Henry G. Manne, a law professor and vigorous opponent of the Nader project, provides the economic argument against interference with traditional corporate obligations and likens the Nader forces to irresponsible student activists. In such a heated climate, it is difficult to get any perspective on what the battle was all about, and E. J. Kahn, Jr., provides an enlightened, nonpolemical discussion of the much publicized shareholders' meeting of May 22, 1970.

THE THREAT TO AMERICAN BUSINESS [1]

Today, . . . let me call your attention to a serious, yet subtle, threat to our American system of free enterprise. I would like to discuss this threat, and the personal responsibility it places upon us, as businessmen, to help counter it.

There are two premises on which I think we can all agree. The first is that our country—by almost any measure —is preeminent in the world. To assert this is not to deny

[1] From the remarks of James M. Roche, then chairman, General Motors Corporation, before the Executive Club of Chicago, March 25, 1971. General Motors Corporation. 767 Fifth Ave. New York 10022. p 1-2, 8-12. mimeo. Reprinted by permission.

our faults. We are still short of achieving many of our national ideals. But neither should we deny the blessings we enjoy as a nation. Most apparent perhaps is our unmatched material well-being. More important, though, are our high levels of education, health, and individual opportunity, and of course our freedoms, the priceless heritage our history has served to enlarge.

A second premise, like the first, is also too little acknowledged. It is that our free competitive economic system has been essential to the achievement and preservation of these national endowments.

These beliefs may seem fundamental to us. Nevertheless, they are questioned by some people in our society today. Notwithstanding that America is the envy and the aspiration of the world, there are those who maintain our economic system is not the best, and ask is there not a better way. Some who question our society and its achievements are young. Some are well-intentioned. Some are sincere.

But there are others. Their final objectives are not what they first profess. Their beliefs, their purposes, run contrary to the principles of the majority of our people. They question many of our institutions, including our economic system. They crusade for radical changes in our system of corporate ownership, changes so drastic that they would all but destroy free enterprise as we know it. Deliberately or not, they are also weakening our free competitive system. . . .

Corporate responsibility is a catchword of the adversary culture that is so evident today. If something is wrong with American society, blame business. Business did not create discrimination in America, but business is expected to eliminate it. Business did not bring about the deterioration of our cities, but business is expected to rebuild them. Business did not create poverty and hunger in our land, but business is expected to eliminate them.

As citizens and Americans, we heartily endorse all these objectives. No thoughtful American can be opposed to equal opportunity, to better housing and education, and to the elimination of poverty from our land. But every thoughtful American must face the fact that new aspirations entail new costs.

We should also recognize that business is not always the best vehicle for their accomplishment, although there is much business can contribute. Business nevertheless is often a convenient scapegoat. But blaming business, or government for that matter, does not excuse us from our own personal responsibility as citizens, as parents, as teachers.

These considerations pose questions which should be much on the mind of every American. Because if our society does not give them a satisfactory answer—and soon—whatever capacity American business does have to influence social change for the better may be severely impaired. Business, burdened by new and unnecessary social costs, may find itself hard-pressed to maintain the economic progress that has so distinguished our history.

The climate of criticism and disparagement has dulled the reputation of business. We read and hear very little that is good about business. Seldom, if ever, is business credited with meeting its basic corporate responsibilities. I submit that American business is fulfilling vital social responsibilities every day—and with great success.

Business does its job when it provides useful jobs at high wages, when it provides useful products at fair prices, when it provides economic growth that produces taxes for government and earnings for stockholders. These are the long-standing social responsibilities of business. Their fulfillment by American business over two centuries has made our America what it is. It is an achievement to be proud of—an achievement to talk about.

Earlier, I said we must be ready to accept change. And business today is expected to respond to the new aspirations of the society it serves. This broad public expectation must be recognized, and these new challenges must be accepted. The costs of many are not prohibitive. For example, the costs of providing greater job opportunities, particularly for minorities, can usually be absorbed in the normal course of business. The same is true of the cost of supporting community and educational activities—business' traditional citizenship role. And for these, we do get value. However, in other areas, for example in the control of pollution, costs are usually substantial. To the extent that they cannot be absorbed, they will raise the price of the product and in turn the overall level of prices in our economy.

As a nation we must be mature enough to face up to the costs involved in meeting our new aspirations. It can mean a weakened competitive position in the world. It can mean higher prices for the consumer, and higher taxes for the citizen. This is no dire forecast. This is already a fact. We are weaker abroad. We have experienced higher prices and higher taxes.

Yet we must not allow this to slow our nation's progress toward the fulfillment of our social aspirations. Our task is to achieve our national social objectives at the least possible cost to our society, to assure full value for the dollars that must be spent, to mount an efficient effort. This is clearly a job where business, and businessmen, have much to contribute. Society must define its objectives and establish priorities. . . .

It is not enough that management should be aware of what benefits—and what costs—are involved in fulfilling social objectives. The owners of American business—and virtually every American has a direct or indirect stake in business—must make the ultimate decision.

In the end, management must be responsive to the wishes of the stockholders. Management is obliged to inform the stockholders as to the problems and the short-term costs as well as the potential long-range benefits of a greater and more direct involvement in social objectives. Then, management must abide by the owners' decision. Through his proxy, every stockholder has that right to decide and must exercise it. After that has been done, management has the responsibility to manage, to preserve and protect the business while leading it in the directions pointed by the stockholders. . . .

The dull cloud of pessimism and distrust which some have cast over free enterprise is impairing the ability of business to meet its basic economic responsibilities—not to mention its capacity to take on newer ones. This, as much as any other factor, makes it urgent that those of us who are in business, who have made business our career, who are justifiably proud of our profession, that we stand up and be counted. It is up to us in the business community to reaffirm our belief in free enterprise.

Business has high goals, large responsibilities, and every incentive to fulfill them. In a climate of understanding, it can continue to provide rising standards of well-being for ourselves and our families. In a climate of encouragement, business can continue to expand job opportunities for the millions of new workers who are entering the labor force. In a climate of confidence, business can continue to offer the wide variety of quality products which consumers demand. In a climate of growth, business can continue to generate the earnings and pay the dividends on which investors, large and small, depend.

This competitive system of ours has achieved results beyond man's imagining. Its potential for further advance is greater than even the achievements in the past. It is time to tell this story with the enthusiasm and strength to match our conviction.

Where the disparagers would diminish freedom, let us enlarge it. Where they would turn other segments of society against us, let us go out and work with government, with the universities, with the press. Let us work together to create a better understanding of what must be done, and how it can best be done. Then let us all join together to get it done —to build the better America to which we all aspire.

This is a job for us in business. We, more than others, appreciate the importance of free enterprise. We, more than others, should therefore feel obliged to work to preserve and protect it.

Let us take this as our mission, as our personal responsibility. For only if we give of ourselves to the fullest, will we draw the full measure of personal satisfaction from the success and the continued progress that I am sure await our nation.

CAMPAIGN GM [2]

Today is announced an effort to develop a new kind of citizenship around an old kind of private government—the large corporation. It is an effort which rises from the shared concern of many citizens over the role of the corporation in American society and the uses of its complex powers. It is an effort which is dedicated toward developing a new constituency for the corporation that will harness these powers for the fulfillment of a broader spectrum of democratic values.

Ours is a corporate society. Corporations produce, process and market most of the goods and services in the nation. They constitute the most powerful, consistent and coordinated power grid that shapes the actions of men in private and public sectors. Yet, far less is known about the actual operations of the giant corporations than any other institution in America, including the national security agencies.

The diverse impacts of corporate actions on citizens, however, are being felt and described in their torment. These impacts are not catalogued in company annual reports whose style of aggregate, numerical evaluation of *company* gains and losses has been mirrored by similarly parochial governmental and scholarly assessments. Instead, corporate imprints are reflecting themselves in growing violence to our air, water and soil environments, in imbalanced

[2] From a statement by Ralph Nader, consumer advocate, announcing Campaign GM to the press, February 7, 1970. Center for Study of Responsive Law. P. O. Box 19367. Washington, D.C. 20036. '70. p 1-8. mimeo. Reprinted by permission.

consumer and producer technologies that harm their users and dehumanize their operators, in the colossal waste and depreciation of consumer goods and services and in the Moloch-like devouring of a society's resources to the detriment of sane and humane allocation of these resources to meet the needs of all the people by superior distribution and innovation. In other negative ways—through the power of avoidance—corporate power centers can condition or determine whether other forces will unjustly prevail over the expression of weaker but more legitimate interests in peace and justice.

For most citizens there can be no rejection of nor escape from the corporate embrace. There can only be submission or control in varying degrees. The choice is between increasing predation or increasing accountability of corporate power to the people. As a bureaucratic structure, the corporation is here to stay and whether it comes in private, public, utility or Comsat-type [Communications Satellite Corporation] dress is less important than the dynamic relationship with its total constituency. The paramount foci should include the establishment of enduring *access* to corporate information, effective *voice* for affected social and individual interests, and thorough *remedy* against unjust treatment.

Throughout the past century, the major forms of curbing the excesses of corporate power have been external pressures and stimuli from government and labor. As confronting organizations, however, government and labor groups did not possess the stamina, motivation and generic nourishment that the corporation displayed to keep its opponents at bay or accommodate their vulnerabilities. While overcoming the regulatory state and adjusting to the narrow goals of organized labor, the modern corporation increased its direct power, and, through an imbalanced use of complex technology, its indirect power over citizens. Now mere inaction, mere forbearance, can wreak havoc on the health, safety and well-being of people.

The corporate quest for control of its operating environment has led industry and commerce to narrow or virtually eliminate the range of quality competition in contrast to nonprice and/or trivia-indentured competition. The same quest has led to endemic violations of antitrust and other economic laws and produced greater and greater concentrations of corporate power. The intricate evolution of the legal structure of the corporation permits the increasing exercise of personal power accompanied by institutional, not personal, responsibility at the most. The corporate shield absorbs the rare enforcement of the law, not the official(s) whose decisions or negligence led to the violation. In addition, the ownership and management of the corporation have become separated and the ease of even the largest investors in exiting reduces any remaining incentive for owners to exercise voice and guide or discipline management. Clearly the gap between corporate performance and corporate responsibility is steadily enlarged by these aforementioned patterns. Just as clearly, a new definition of the corporation's constituency and its activation is needed.

With its massive size and pervasiveness, General Motors is a leading candidate for the attentions of its assertive constituency—consumers, labor, dealers, suppliers, insurance companies and all citizens who experience the forced consumption of its air pollution and other environmental spillages. Nearly a million and a half of these citizens and institutions are shareholders in the company. In theory they own the company, in fact they have about the same rights as the owner of company debentures. The procedures, the information, the organization, the manpower and the funds are management's to deploy. But the fiction of shareholder democracy continues to plague the reality. By highlighting the fiction a new reality can be born that will tame the corporate tiger.

And verily, a tiger is General Motors. By virtue of the engines it produces and the plants it operates, the company contributes about 35 percent of the nation's air pollution by tonnage. Its *hourly* average gross, around the clock, of

$2.4 million has not discouraged the company from spending last year less than $15 million on research and development for less polluting engines. Grossing more than any single governmental budget, except that of the USA and the USSR, GM, with its 1969 gross of some $24 billion, still cannot find the will to build the greatly safer automobiles that can be built economically by free engineers. The company continues to lead the way in designs that pile up enormous and avoidable property damage in low-speed (under 10 mph) collisions and increase its aftermarket replacement sales as a result. The company is a charter member of the highway lobby that has opposed successfully the development of mass transit systems and pushed highways through cities and suburbs in the most indiscriminate manner of land use planning. The market power that is synonymous with GM has propelled the industry toward attenuated competition or collusion over design and marketing practices. Innovation has been creatively stayed to the consumer's harm and economic detriment. GM's huge financing arm, General Motors Acceptance Corporation, according to congressional testimony, engages in deceptive, usurious and exploitive practices in its service to the parent corporation. Secrecy, obfuscation and contracts of adhesion characterize the techniques used to render consumers impotent in remedy for their complaints. These are only the surface references to GM's imprint but they suggest a ferocity of acquisitiveness which could render an optimist euphoric at the prospect of transforming such motivational velocities *for* man instead of *against* man. What is emerging from closer study of companies such as General Motors is that the most intractable obstacles to change *for* man are not technical at all but are more often associated with rigidities of a bureaucratic and personal nature rather than an economic incapacity or loss. The half century of delay in installing a collapsible steering column was quite probably due to the vested interest of an authoritarian psychology than to the more conventionally adduced reasons. When the decision was made for the

1967 model cars that the collapsible steering column was "in," it was finally decided that in any collision between man and column, prudence dictated that the column should give, not the man's rib cage. This microcosmic episode illustrates the enormous power in the hands of those who decide manufacturing priorities and product designs (the ramrodding steering column is estimated to have fatally injured over 200,000 Americans since 1900). They need assistance in making such decisions along the entire continuum of impacts on people. A few years ago, the company produced many advertisements with the headline "GM IS PEOPLE." It is time to amend the caption to "GM IS FOR PEOPLE." In addition, GM is continually violating laws, including air pollution and safety laws, and it is time for shareholders to voice their concern here. For as has been said, shareholders are harmed as consumers and citizens by the very activities that they own in part.

Campaign GM will appeal to the nearly million and a half shareholders of the company. It will appeal to these shareholders as citizens and consumers, victims of air and water pollution, congested and inefficient transportation and rocketing repair bills for shoddy workmanship.

I am informed that a new organization called the Project on Corporate Responsibility, record holder presently of twelve shares of GM stock, is mailing to its company three shareholder resolutions with the request that they be included in the proxy statement to be sent by GM to its shareholders in April, preparatory for the annual meeting in Detroit on May 22, 1970.

The first of these resolutions proposes an amendment to GM's charter which would limit the business purposes of the corporation to those purposes which are not detrimental to the public health, safety and welfare.

The second resolution proposes that a shareholders' committee for corporate responsibility be established. This committee, to be appointed jointly by representatives from GM, the campaign committee and the United Auto Workers, would prepare a study on the corporate impact of GM on its workers, the environment, transport safety and efficiency and the public welfare. It will recommend new priorities for the corporation to pursue. The committee will render a report to the shareholders in time for shareholder action at the next meeting. To permit such a task to be accomplished, the committee would have access to all of GM's files.

The third resolution proposes to amend the bylaws of the corporation to increase the size of the Board of Directors from twenty-four to twenty-seven members. The purpose of this action, as explained in the statement supporting the resolution, would be to make room on the Board for three representatives of the public without displacing anyone now on the Board of Directors.

Three knowledgeable and public-spirited citizens have agreed to stand for election as public representatives on the Board. They are Professor René Dubos, Miss Betty Furness and the Rev. Channing Phillips. . . . The assumption to the Board of these three Americans and the adoption of the aforementioned resolutions will go a long way toward making the days of GM executives less daily and less inimical to the short- and long-run public interest.

This campaign will seek to win public and shareholder support for these resolutions and candidates. The drive will be run by the Campaign to Make GM Responsible Committee, a Washington-based organization with four coordinators—Philip Moore, executive secretary, Geoffrey Cowan, Joseph N. Onek and John C. Esposito. The coordinators will undertake a nationwide effort to raise many of the issues relating to the public impact of GM's private decision making.

A basic thrust of the campaign will be alerting and informing the public about their omnipresent neighbor—General Motors—and how it behaves. It will ask citizens to make their views known to both shareholders and management. It will go to institutions that own GM stock and, if they decline to respond, the constituents of those institutions will be contacted. The campaign will reach to the universities and their students and faculty, to the banks and their depositors and fiduciaries, to churches and their congregations, to insurance companies and their policyholders, to union and company pension funds and their membership and to other investors. Not only is everyone affected by General Motors, whether a car owner or not, but almost everyone could exert some influence on some aspect of the company's operations. The totality of such influence may be productive of a sustained momentum. At its annual meeting on May 22, 1970, GM may be the host for a great public debate on the giant corporation rather than a wooden recital of aggregate financial data. Putting the people back into "people's capitalism," as the New York Stock Exchange once phrased it before small investors were desired to go out of style, is no easy task. But then it never was for any period in our history. Increasingly the looming issue is that the choices no longer include the luxury of deferral. Rather they demand the urgency of unyielding reform.

GOOD FOR GENERAL MOTORS? [3]

The outcome of Ralph Nader's "Project for Corporate Responsibility" campaign against General Motors Corporation is a foregone conclusion. . . . GM's management will defeat, by a lopsided margin, the two shareholder proposals cleared by the Securities and Exchange Commission. But it should not be a day of rejoicing by friends of free enterprise. The resolutions probably will receive more votes than any shareholder proposal opposed by management has ever won.

The Project for Corporate Responsibility strikes us as more a stroke of propaganda than a serious effort to have shareholders participate effectively in policy making. None-

[3] From article by Henry G. Manne, Kenan Professor of Law in the Department of Political Science at the University of Rochester. *Barron's.* 50:1+. My. 18, '70. Reprinted by permission.

theless, as a measure of popular feeling on the subject of corporate freedom, it is highly revealing. Not even Ralph Nader could have elicited such publicity for a preordained failure if the groundwork had not been well laid by years of unrelenting anticorporate propaganda, emanating from so-called liberal politicians and disaffected academics. It is no accident that the turmoil-ridden universities are the chief targets of vote solicitation in this odd proxy fight.

For years anticorporate polemicists have been ministering to the imagined ills of American industry. Whole schools of thought have been built around one or another contrived issue involving large publicly-held corporations. Ideas like corporate responsibility, shareholder democracy, corporate constitutionalism and other nonmarket theories are a focal point of modern liberal thought. The need for "some" regulation of corporate giants is taken as matter-of-factly by most "well-informed" Americans today as the need for a cancer cure. And in some circles it would be almost more welcome. Now we are beginning to see the effects of these views on public confidence in the corporate sector. No public figure has stepped forward to defend corporations as natural, desirable outgrowths of a private property, free exchange system. And the belief that all is not well with the system has gradually spread from the anti-free-market intellectual circles of Adolf Berle and John Kenneth Galbraith into the public domain.

There has been a spate of activist disruptions of shareholder meetings and some noisy picketing this year, and the pace will quicken. But the public's imagination has been stirred chiefly by the Project for Corporate Responsibility. This reflects the Project's close tie to Ralph Nader and the identity of its first major target. For General Motors symbolizes everything today's critics of capitalism and private property detest. It is the largest nonregulated, private corporation in the world (which allows nonsensical comparisons like "General Motors' gross revenue is greater than the revenue of any government except that of the United States and that

of the Soviet Union"); it makes automobiles (which allegedly are ugly, pollute the atmosphere, kill 50,000 people a
year and cause traffic jams); and turns out military equipment. One could also add to this list such intellectual gar-
barge as claims that General Motors does not produce a
small car because it controls buyers and makes more money
on large cars; that it could easily put all other automobile
companies out of business and would do so if not prevented
by the antitrust laws; that it practices planned obsolescence
so that consumers will have to pay more for their too-fre-
quent trade-ins; that GM keeps its dealers in near servitude
by the threat of arbitrary franchise cancellations. What better target could Nader seek? What company could already
be more softened up for the kill?

It might be well, nonetheless, to examine the proposals
cleared by the SEC for mandatory inclusion in General
Motors' proxy materials. On the surface they may seem no
more significant or threatening than the Gilbert brothers'
perennial pinpricks. [Lewis D. Gilbert and John Gilbert,
often referred to as "professional stockholders" and "corporate gadflies," have for many years attended shareholders'
meetings across the country and questioned executives on
management policies.—Ed.] But closer examination reveals
a potential for real harm to the US capitalist system. The
first proposal would require the addition of three "public"
members to GM's board of directors; the second calls for the
establishment of a "General Motors shareholders' committee
for corporate responsibility." In this fashion, Nader maintains, corporations would become accountable "to the people," who would gain access to information, assert an
effective voice in corporate policies and insist on remedies
for unjust treatment. But these goals represent a philosophy
so antagonistic to notions of private property and individual
responsibility that their real significance should be exposed.

The access to information which the Project for Corporate Responsibility demands is no "full disclosure" of the
SEC variety. What this phrase means in the current vernac-

ular is that every important decision made by the company should first be examined publicly after the fashion of political issues like defense spending, tax policy or welfare programs. The implication of such an idea is that important corporate policy debates will be carried into the streets, just as has occurred, with much the same backing, in American universities.

The goal is not publicity for publicity's sake, since "the people" are to have an "effective voice" in corporate policy. Student radicals have made very clear what they mean by such a voice. They mean that they will have their way and no other. Similarly, no one should be misled into believing that three directors will satisfy Nader and the legions of corporate foes who have rallied to his cause. Obviously three directors would not provide "an effective voice"; only a majority could do that. How, then, can Project spokesmen allege that three directors will give "the people" (which presumably does not include General Motors' almost 1.5 million shareholders) an effective voice? They probably don't, since reasoned debate is not what they really want. Their aim is not parliamentary give-and-take, but power.

This is not to suggest that Nader and his close friends propose bombing corporate facilities or rioting in the streets. The precedent they have in mind now is probably Nader's colossal, single-handed political victory in the field of auto safety. The fact remains, however, that many activists do think mainly in terms of amassing sufficient public protest to coerce politicans or businessmen, in order to stave off violence, into granting their demands. The method has not been unsuccessful lately.

But let us move on to another question. How will the public representatives be selected after Nader has lost the power simply to name three people immediately acceptable to the left as appropriate voices of "the people"? Plainly the Project for Corporate Responsibility has no claim to political legitimacy or to represent anyone with an interest in General Motors and its products. Perhaps the advocates of the proposal anticipate that political parties will support competing candidates for these positions. Perhaps—but I doubt it.

Actually the old ideas of corporate democracy play no role in Nader's thinking. True democratic representation of shareholder interests is the last thing he wants. Lewis D. Gilbert must seem more eccentric to Nader than he does to some members of the corporate establishment. After all, the Gilbert brothers recognize that the property interests at stake in the corporate system are those of the shareholders, and they never propose anything designed to shake the foundation of the system or compromise legitimate shareholder interests.

Nor should we be misled by the fact that the Project is simply using the available legal means to gain its ends. It may seem innocent enough. After all, other outsiders have engaged corporate managers in fights for control, which is what the campaign amounts to. And the Gilberts and others have had their say on the floor at annual meetings, which is what the Project people demand. But let there be no mistake. The Project represents an abuse of traditional legal norms just as mass demonstrations, with uncontrollable violence, may abuse conventionable legal ideas of free speech.

Traditional corporate rules were designed for a system in which there exists a popular consensus about the rights of human beings to own property, and about the self-interest with which individuals risked their savings in profit-oriented ventures. The old rules make sense in that context—and in no other. If those who would destroy the private wealth of others are not restrained, the rules will have to be changed —to the ultimate detriment of us all.

Another revealing question to ask of Project proponents is what criteria they propose to use in their policy making. If they intend to abandon the objective standard of profit maximization, what will they substitute? Is it to be clean environment at any price? Perhaps Nader's book title, *Unsafe at Any Speed*, was prophetic. After all, that includes zero. And what about other controversial issues with which public directors would be concerned? How should they settle matters of free trade versus protectionism; or "fair" wages versus inflation; or dividends versus charity, to cite a few? To ask the question is to make clear that they have no valid yardsticks for settling such issues.

Those who fear economic freedom have never understood the tremendous benefits of the price mechanism. And not having grasped this much, they have scant idea of the complexities involved in determining priorities and "properly" allocating resources. Inevitably they assume that a clear conscience and a moral motive will be sufficient. If it were only so!

There is a further economic problem connected with the goals of less air pollution and more auto safety. Regardless of the desirability of legislation for such purposes, the idea of seeking to coerce one company to adopt measures not demanded of its competitors runs counter to the whole ideal of free, competitive markets operating under a rule of law. Clearly these are matters to be studied and dealt with by government for an entire industry or for all industrial concerns. General Motors has been singled out because of its political vulnerability, not because it is the most egregious offender or because it makes sense to go after one company at a time. . . .

It is easy to see why a group like Nader's can propose things more preposterous even than those which usually come out of Washington. Politicians must accept responsibility for what they propose. And anyone urging legislation which would raise the price of automobiles and lower the price of auto stocks would surely have to answer to a significant group of "the people." Nader, contrariwise, occupies the same position as student activists in the university. They demand all manner of changes which no rational administrator could ever propose or adopt. Administrators, after all, must accept responsibility for their decisions, while the demanders stand to lose nothing by being wrong. Power without individual responsibility is fundamental to a totalitarian system. But it is not too attractive to those who wish to live in freedom.

Leftist folklore holds that corporate directors constitute a self-perpetuating oligarchy, wholly independent of realistic constraints by millions of widely diffused, small shareholders. But if that were so, it is very doubtful that Americans would continue year after year to pour billions of dollars into such a system. The truth is that every shareholder in a US corporation has a restraining influence over his corporate managers exactly commensurate with the size of his holdings. And since the latter precisely reflect the amount of wealth he is willing to risk in the venture, the equation of power and individual responsibility is perfect.

Political models of corporate behavior have failed because they could not comprehend the essential economic role of secondary capital markets in transmitting shareholder power to the managers. The critical point is that any sale of shares of a company's stock determines precisely the appropriate degree of decline in the stock's price relative to other stocks. The greater the shareholder dissatisfaction, the lower the price of the company's stock relative to that of other companies. As prices decline, other market phenomena begin to operate, or threaten to; hence corporate managers are constrained to behave precisely as classical market theory suggests they should.

This model explains in large measure the incredible success of the American corporate system as a device for administering the private investment funds of tens of millions of people, most of whom are said to be powerless. The truth is that the market mercilessly visits on corporate managers the full brunt of shareholder preference, and that preference has yet to be for anything other than the highest possible value for the shares.

In 1934 Congress apparently concluded that corporations were failing their shareholders because they were not democratic enough. Consequently the lawmakers adopted schemes of full disclosure, proxy regulation and the referendum device known as the shareholder proposal rule. The last of these was actually feared most by the business community; hence the SEC, itself sensitive to the charge that the rule might be used by crackpots, severely limited its area of applicability.

The Nader proposals, however, posed difficult political problems for the Commission. No proposal as radical as either of the two accepted had ever gotten through the SEC. But Nader is a popular hero, and the SEC didn't want thousands of his followers on its neck. Thus the decision to allow two of his nine proposals to go into the proxy materials bears all the earmarks of a political compromise. Obviously General Motors' shareholders have already been sacrificed in some measure to the political realities of the day. And while the eternal hope is that "this too shall pass," the anticorporate notions coming from the left continue to mount.

The irony in all this is that the business community thus far has been unable to find its voice. Too many businessmen show either lack of comprehension of the free enterprise system or a belief in some of the rhetoric of the left. It is as though they admit to being anachronisms who do not want to risk being ridiculed by the younger generation for still defending capitalism. The proper answer to Nader is not a meek, "We'll try to do better." It should be a booming, "No one in the world has ever done so well."

But this is the kind of doctrinal confidence which intelligent people develop only if they believe in the underlying logic. And the logical lessons of capitalism are reaching fewer and fewer people. How many businessmen realize that only an insignificant fraction of US college students today are even exposed to the arguments of morality and welfare traditionally made for a free exchange system. The typical academic approach to the American business establishment is more likely to be critical, harping and snide. Ridicule and hatred of the competitive, private property system are taught relentlessly to vast numbers of university students.

The cadres marching on American business have trained at Berkeley, Wisconsin, Cornell and hundreds of other schools. The propaganda which has set them in motion has been going on a lot longer. Isn't it incredible that American businessmen and financiers are still so naive as to think they are being charitable when they support institutions and individuals who, measure by measure, move us all closer to the end of the capitalist system?

WE LOOK FORWARD TO SEEING YOU NEXT YEAR [4]

E. J. KAHN, JR.

DETROIT. Macomb County, which takes in part of this city, is known as, among other things, the Hothouse Rhubarb Capital of the World, but when I got here on the afternoon of May 21st, the day before the annual stockholders' meeting of the General Motors Corporation, and went around to the G.M. headquarters building to look in on management, tranquillity prevailed; the most exciting visible development was a new space-saving Frigidaire washer-dryer in a ground-floor showroom, which somebody, presumably after thorough meditation, had dubbed the Skinny Mini. The outward calm notwithstanding, many G.M. executives were apprehensive. This is the year, after all, when youthful activists are looking hard at big corporations; a month earlier, the annual meeting of the Honeywell corporation, in Minneapolis, had had to be cancelled after fourteen raucous minutes. Not that the G.M. management really had to worry about its shareholders' voting down any of its recommendations. In the narrowest squeak management had ever

4 Reprint of article by E. J. Kahn, Jr., author and member of the *New Yorker* staff. *New Yorker.* 46:40-2+. Je. 20, '70. Reprinted by permission; © 1970 The New Yorker Magazine, Inc.

encountered (last year, on a perennial proposal to limit executive compensation, no doubt inspired by the fact that G.M. currently has six officers who, in salary and bonus, get over half a million dollars a year each), 92.8 per cent of the vote backed company policy (no limit). Two hundred and eighty-six million-odd shares of General Motors common stock are outstanding, the majority owned by institutions that can regularly be counted on to vote with management. Among these are several foundations established by former G.M. panjandrums—the Charles F. Kettering Foundation, for instance, with 850,000 shares; the Alfred P. Sloan Foundation, with 1,540,000; and the Charles Stewart Mott Foundation, with 2,700,000. The Mott Foundation and the Mott family and Mr. Mott personally—at ninety-five, he is the senior General Motors director, having been on the board since 1917—own a total of four million shares, which even at today's low market price are worth a quarter of a billion dollars.

Still, this year's meeting came at a time when General Motors was beset by all sorts of problems. Business was off; first-quarter per-share earnings had dropped from $1.82 to $1.21. On the stock market, G.M. shares were at their lowest point since early 1963. Walter Reuther had died. Negotiations for a new contract with the United Auto Workers, covering most of the company's four hundred and forty-two thousand hourly-rate employees, were soon to start, and even under the existing contract, because of a rise in the cost of living, the corporation would shortly be obliged to pay out an additional twenty-six cents an hour. President Nixon had asked Congress to impose a new tax on leaded gasoline. Secretary of the Interior Hickel had just suggested that the motor industry was too fecund. "What this country needs is a Pill for the automobile," he said.

And, to cap it all, there was Ralph Nader. The author of "Unsafe at Any Speed," whose impact on General Motors' equanimity had already been as jarring as a pothole, had in February spoken out in favor of a consumer group called the Project on Corporate Responsibility, and had predicted that at this year's annual meeting "General Motors may be the host to a great public debate on the giant corporation rather than a wooden recital of aggregate financial data." He had also said, "And verily, a tiger is General Motors." Nader was not technically a member of the Project, but he was acknowledged as its guru. He was also the guiding light of a Project enterprise called the Campaign to Make General Motors Responsible—Campaign GM, for short. Four young Washington lawyers were the Campaign's official organizers, and to qualify for admittance to the May meeting they had jointly bought twelve shares of G.M. common. They thought that General Motors should engage in open debate with them on the environment (one-third of the nation's air pollution, they asserted, was attributable to G.M. cars), on safety (many of the country's fifty thousand annual automobile fatalities, they contended, could be blamed on car manufacturers), and on discrimination against minorities (of General Motors' thirteen thousand franchised dealers, they said, only seven were non-white, and on the huge G.M. payroll there were precious few white-collar employees whose collars were not surmounted by white faces). When General Motors refused to voluntarily incorporate nine Campaign GM proposals in its pre-meeting proxy statement —among the nine were proposals dealing with pollution, safety, consumer warranties, and mass transit—the young lawyers appealed to the Securities and Exchange Commission, which ruled that two of the proposals would have to be presented to the stockholders. One advocated the establishment of a Shareholders' Committee for Corporate Responsibility—a consumer watchdog body operating within the framework of the corporation. The other advocated that the General Motors board, which has twenty-three members, be augmented by three directors representing the public at large. Campaign GM even had a slate ready: an environmentalist, Professor René Dubos, of the Rockefeller University; a black man, the Reverend Mr. Channing Phillips, whose name was put in nomination for the Presidency at the 1968 Democratic National Convention; and a woman, Betty Furness, who during the Johnson Administration had represented consumers at the White House.

Last year, only seven hundred and twenty-four of General Motors' one million three hundred and sixty-eight thousand stockholders attended the annual meeting in Cobo Hall, Detroit's counterpart of the Coliseum. Anticipating a larger turnout this time, even though there were twenty thousand fewer shareholders, the company had arranged to transmit the proceedings by closed-circuit television to an overflow room. I went over to Cobo Hall the day before the meeting. On display in the lobby was a Car of the Year—a 1970 Ford Torino. Impressed by Detroit's independence, I moved along upstairs to a room where some of the Campaign GM people—many of them wearing red-and-white buttons that said "Tame G.M."—had set up shop. The majority of them were Harvard men; a notable exception was a young graduate of Whittier, in California. Working as a group, they had been trying to round up the votes of colleges and universities that own General Motors stock, and they had succeeded in corralling Tufts' ninety-three hundred, Brown's forty-seven hundred, and Amherst's thirty-seven thousand (for at least one of the proposals). Yale, with eighty-six thousand; Williams, with twenty-one thousand; Stanford, with twenty-four thousand; Swarthmore, with twenty-two hundred; and the Rockefeller University, with sixty-three thousand, were abstaining, which in Campaign GM eyes was a moral victory, but Harvard had decided to vote its two hundred and eighty-seven thousand shares for management despite pressure from students, faculty, and alumni. The Campaign GM people were very disappointed over Harvard, but their spirits were lifted by the arrival in Cobo Hall of a distinguished Harvard professor—George Wald, the Nobel Prize-winning biologist. Professor Wald not long before had bought ten shares of G.M. stock, so that he could participate in the meeting. "Ralph Nader called me and asked if I would consider becoming one of the three public nominees for the board," he told me. "But I just don't have it in my image to be a director of General Motors. I was in Cleveland not long ago and heard about a G.M. plant that makes Sheridan tanks, and after I bought my ten shares I got a letter from the chairman welcoming me to the family and mentioning a long list of G.M. products but nowhere alluding to the tanks. Are they *ashamed* of producing the Sheridan tank?"

The stockholders' meeting was scheduled for 2 P.M., but five hours before that Cobo Hall was astir with dozens of trim-haired, dark-suited, white-shirted General Motors men, who nervously hovered about, all looking like the sort of person one might meet at a dinner and not recognize the next day. At the curb outside, a solitary Detroit police car was parked. Another Ford. Guards were everywhere, some in plain-clothes, some wearing "Peerless Security" shoulder patches. As the morning went on, more and more of the actors who would be playing leading roles in the afternoon's pageant materialized. Here, chatting together in a corridor, were two celebrated *enfants terribles* of the annual-meeting circuit— Lewis Gilbert and Wilma Soss. Mrs. Soss had a broken foot and was in a wheelchair; she was wearing a headpiece fashioned of paper play money and a large brooch topped by a gilded gadfly. Gilbert remarked to her that in his opinion Betty Furness should stick to opening refrigerator doors. Mrs. Soss characterized Ralph Nader as "the architect of unemployment" and said he was afraid to come to Detroit. (He didn't come to the meeting; he has a seventeen-million-dollar invasion-of-privacy suit pending against General Motors, and no doubt his attorneys had urged him to stay away lest he do or say something that could jeopardize his case.) Not far away, perhaps the most *terrible* of the annual-meeting *enfants* was warming up. This was Evelyn Y. Davis, in white tights and a black bathing suit, with a sash reading "Miss Air Pollution" across her chest. Mrs. Davis was carrying a gilded gas mask and an American flag, and was distributing press releases about having divorced her husband. Beyond her were young people selling copies of the *Militant*. Here, too, suitcase in hand, just off a plane, was Stewart Rawlings Mott, the thirty-two-year-old son of G.M.'s ninety-five-year-old patriarch. The younger Mott owns two thousand shares of G.M. outright and is one of the beneficiaries of trust funds containing some seven hundred thousand shares. These provide him with a million dollars in dividends annually, and he passes much of this along to liberal politicians and proponents of population control. Stewart Mott said he was not affiliated with Campaign GM and disagreed with some of its tactics, but he intended to vote his two thousand shares for its two proposals. Here, furthermore, standing on line to get a ticket to the meeting, was a bushy-bearded Michigan State student wearing a sweatshirt, khakis, moccasins, and a rumpled Army field jacket with a red-fist strike symbol stencilled on the back. "I like this kind of involvement," he said. "I got here early this morning and took a little rest in the basement, and when I walked upstairs it just blew General Motors' minds. This one G.M. guy came up as if he was my best buddy and put his arm around my shoulder and asked could he help me, and I got the feeling he wanted to help me out the front door."

At eleven-thirty, the Campaign GM operatives, who throughout the morning had been registering people who wanted to vote anti-management proxies, held a final pep rally upstairs in Cobo Hall. The principal speaker was Robert Townsend, the author of "Up the Organization," who was wearing one of those waistline-reducing, or down-the-corporation, belts. Mr. Townsend said that when he was running the Avis rent-a-car company he had found General Motors to be far and away the most arrogant automobile manufacturer. "If I were making a profit of five million dollars a day, I'd probably be arrogant, too," he said. "The only way you can have any effect on General Motors is not to buy any of their cars until they produce a clean one—and they could do it in three years. Their chairman, Jim

Roche, has the power to call in his people right now and tell them that he's going to cut his annual advertising budget from two hundred and forty million to forty million —our opening campaign at Avis cost only six million a year, but I'm allowing them forty, because they're more inept—and earmark it all for just one advertising message: 'General Motors is going to spend four hundred million dollars in two years to wipe out air pollution.' His people would fall in a heap on the floor, and then they would say they couldn't possibly do it in two years. Then he could compromise and give them three years."

The doors to the meeting room were opened at twelve-thirty, and by two there wasn't an empty seat. The total attendance, including those in the overflow room, was over three thousand. The nineteen attending members of the G.M. board of directors were seated in the front of the audience, facing a dais for the G.M. chairman and several subsidiary officers, including the president of the company— but not all the way up front; the first row was occupied by a shoulder-to-shoulder phalanx of younger executives, possibly an animated bumper to cushion their elders against accidents. A few minutes before two, a very old man with a white mustache and marvellous white eyebrows moved slowly and erectly to the directors' section. It was Charles S. Mott, and the shareholders nearby gave him a standing ovation. But the indisputable star of the drama was James M. Roche, the chairman of the board, who, precisely at two, gavelled the meeting to order. It was six hours and twenty-five minutes later—the longest of any General Motors stockholders' meeting by nearly two hours—that he had his first chance to sit down. Patient and all but unflappable, as well as durable, the sixty-three-year-old white-haired Mr. Roche looked as though he would make a superb grandfather.

The first, and tamest, part of the meeting was devoted chiefly to a routine management report from Mr. Roche— with occasional impromptu footnotes from Mrs. Soss and Mrs. Davis. The chairman also presented his fellow-directors to the stockholders; though the audience was enjoined to refrain from applause until all had bowed, Mr. Mott evoked another spontaneous accolade. General Motors stockholders love to be reminded of the good old days. Then—to the groans of some of the Campaign GM contingent—came a twenty-five-minute General Motors propaganda film; most of it, interestingly, dwelt on G.M.'s noble deeds in precisely those environmental and racial areas that Campaign GM had wanted to talk about but that the corporation had said were irrelevant to the occasion. After requesting that nobody bring up a personal matter (e.g., a car that didn't work), Mr. Roche asked for approval of the minutes of the previous annual meeting. He got it, and after some discussion about whether two former directors had quit the board voluntarily or because the anti-trust division of the Justice Department had forced them to, Mrs. Davis seized a microphone near her and accused Roche of being responsible for the bear market. Scattered boos, but whether the audience was booing the market or booing her for blaming its decline on General Motors was impossible to tell. In any event, when she went on to describe Mr. Roche as "stupid," he cut off her amplification, and when she continued to shriek imprecations into the dead mike, a man moved that she be thrown out. Roche said evenly that General Motors had never done that, and invited the maker of the motion to reconsider. There was no second, and Mrs. Davis remained free to wave her flag and her voice.

Mr. Roche then asked for nominations to the board of directors, and a young man arose, friendly as a puppy. "Hello, Mr. Roche," he began. "How are you today? The movie was too long. Hello, stockholders, too." He said that he had seen a lot of minority-group faces on the movie screen but few in the room; that he walked around Detroit a lot and had got carbon monoxide hooked up to his hemoglobin in a very tight bind; and that he wanted to nominate for the board of directors an immigrant Armenian named Martin Jankowski, who had been adopted by some Polish folks, and who worked for General Motors and played baseball, too. Roche broke in to ask for the nominee's name. "His Polish name?" asked the nominator. The chairman ruled him out of order.

Somebody else moved that the nominations be closed, but before that could be voted on a man named Albert R. Appleby, chairman of the Los Angeles chapter of Business Executives Move for Vietnam Peace, sneaked in a nomination for Stewart Mott. The Campaign GM crowd cheered; the aficionados of the senior Mott sat on their hands. To second the nomination, Appleby brought on George Wald. It probably didn't matter much that Appleby identified him as an M.I.T. professor rather than a Harvard one; Mr. Roche seemed not to have heard of the Nobel laureate in any context, and although Professor Wald's remarks were no more discursive and a good deal more rational than most of the other words that had been uttered from the floor up to then, the chairman almost at once started to rein him in. Unflustered, Professor Wald promised to be brief and went on to remark how he had been in Cleveland not long before and had heard about a factory that made Sheridan tanks, and . . . Mr. Roche cut off his microphone. Mrs. Soss —calling Stewart Mott "Stephen," and wrongly identifying him as his father's grandson—presently broke in to say that the nominee drove a Volkswagen and was "wet behind the ears." Mr. Roche, who had earlier said that he would tolerate no personal remarks, did not cut her off, but he did remonstrate mildly with Mrs. Davis when, brandishing her flag, she demanded to know why the thirty-two-year-old Mott wasn't in the Army. As for Mott himself, he declined to run, gave an abbreviated version of some remarks he had prepared, and then asked the chair for a summary of General Motors' attitude toward the war. Mr. Roche replied that as long as the war continued, G.M. would provide the country with whatever its elected representatives said they needed. "I think we all deplore the war," he said. "I think we would all like to see the hostilities in Indo-China brought to a successful conclusion at the earliest possible time." The nominations for the board were then closed, and those present who had not already voted by proxy filled out ballots.

Then came a surprise. The chair recognized a man who said that he had to leave early and wanted to read a seconding speech he had prepared on behalf of Campaign GM's proposal for a Shareholder's Committee, even though the proposal itself hadn't yet come up. The man was Leonard Woodcock, the brand-new chief of the United Auto Workers. He was indulging in what, under parliamentary procedure, might have been called a Point of I'll-See-You-Later-at-the-Bargaining-Table. It was the first time a president of the U.A.W. had ever attended—let alone spoken at—a G.M. annual meeting, and Mr. Roche gave Mr. Woodcock free rein. "I must confess I never knew your meetings were so much fun," the labor leader said, and went on to make his seconding speech. Then the meeting turned to a discussion in which much—probably too much—was made of the fact that Mr. Roche had earned six hundred and fifty-five thousand dollars from General Motors in 1969. Lewis Gilbert did unbend long enough to say, evoking a fleeting smile from the chairman, "There's one day in the year when you earn the money, and that's when you preside at this annual meeting." Curiously, although everyone in the hall had had access to the G.M. proxy statement, nobody inquired why George Russell, whose only present title is Member of the Finance Committee of the Board, was paid even more than Roche in 1969—a total of seven hundred and fifteen thousand dollars.

It was 5:06 P.M. before the proposal on the Shareholders' Committee came up formally. Whether by calculation or not, the chairman had managed things so adroitly that much of the audience was by then impatient to go home. Betty Furness got the floor, and had barely opened her mouth when she yielded graciously to a challenge from Mrs. Soss. Then Mrs. Davis—without anybody's yielding to her—

broke in. Soon another lady shareholder was recognized and was allowed to deliver a rambling tirade against Ralph Nader, and even to suggest, if I understood her correctly, that if Nader's youthful followers would stop drinking and taking drugs there would be fewer splendid General Motors cars involved in accidents. Not long after she finally braked herself, a male stockholder told Mr. Roche that by repeatedly calling upon certain predictable filibusterers in the room he was in effect conducting a filibuster himself. At 6:33 P.M., Mrs. Soss announced that she had to go home to her husband. This was widely greeted as just about the best news of the day. Shortly thereafter, discussion was closed and a vote on the Shareholders' Committee was taken.

Then began a debate on Campaign GM's proposal to add an environmentalist, a black, and a woman consumer to the board. The chairman came the closest he did all day to losing his cool when Campaign GM put on Miss Barbara Williams, a young black woman studying law at U.C.L.A. "Why are there no blacks on the board?" she asked. "Because none of them have been elected," Roche replied. "I expected better of you," Miss Williams said. She repeated the question, and this time he said, "No black has been nominated, and no black has been elected." Her voice trembling, she asked it a third time. "I have answered the question," said Roche. "You have failed not only the shareholders but the country," said Miss Williams. She changed her tack: Why were there no women on the board? "Our directors are selected on the basis of their ability to make a contribution to the success of General Motors," said Roche. Miss Williams said, "You have not adequately answered those questions," and sat down, to cheers, whistles, and a cry of "Right on!"—conceivably the first time the chairman had ever heard the phrase live.

The discussion of that proposal sputtered to a halt at seven-thirty, and was followed by numerous random questions about General Motors' involvement in South Africa and the alleged exploitation of women in Oldsmobile ads, and then by some thoughts on front-end styling by a share-holder who said, "The purpose of the front end of a car is to run into other cars, people, air, and bugs." In due course, the results of the balloting were announced. Management had won handily on every proposal. The highest number of votes received by any of the directors nominated by the board was 237,575,150, and the lowest number 237,568,381—a discrepancy that may remain forever unexplained. On the proposal for a Shareholders' Committee, 61,794 stockholders gave 6,361,299 votes to Campaign GM—a whopping total in most leagues, but in General Motors' ballpark a mere 2.73 per cent of the actual total. On the proposal to add the three directors, it was 53,495 stockholders, 5,691,130 votes, and 2.44 per cent. A law professor made a few brief closing remarks on behalf of Campaign GM, complimenting Mr. Roche on his courtesy and stamina, adding a special tribute to the undauntable Miss Williams, and winding up, "Mr. Roche, we look forward to seeing you next year." Whatever Mr. Roche, who has less than two years to go before retire-ment, may have felt about that, he, too, was gallantry per-sonified. He thanked the shareholders—in remarks that had been prepared before the session began—for "a most grati-fying expression of confidence," and added, "We leave this meeting more determined than ever to fulfill our responsi-bilities. . . . There is much more that pulls us together than pushes us apart. . . . Join us, help us, so that we may work constructively together." It was 8:25 P.M., the single word "Adjournment" was flashed onto the movie screen, and the longest stockholders' meeting in General Motors' history was over.

IV. THE CORPORATE FAMILY

EDITOR'S INTRODUCTION

It is possible that in the conflict between the corporation and its detractors those who make up the corporation have been neglected. Corporations employ millions of people from apprentices to executives. Whatever the responsibility of the corporation should be, it is carried out by management. Management comes mainly from business schools, and the first article in this section—Andrew Tobias' review of an irreverent book about the Harvard Business School—indicates what businessmen are made of.

That the executive has his problems is detailed in a selection by William M. Evan, and next Arthur J. Goldberg makes a plea to expand top management for its own good and the good of the country. Films usually picture corporation directors as tall, white males; that image may still hold true for the majority of executives, but an article from *Time* and an excerpt from *Black Enterprise* quoted in the *Congressional Record* reflect a new pattern in which women and blacks are no longer eliminated from consideration for top-level jobs. The final three articles center on the role of those below the top. Lucia Mouat discusses the reporting of corporate misfeasance, Tom Wicker makes a case for management's considering the happiness of workers on the job, and Reginald Stuart writes of giving the worker an opportunity to talk directly to top management in annual "jobholder meetings."

THE EDUCATION OF CORPORATE MANAGERS [1]

There are three kinds of people in the world: Those who

[1] From "What Goes On at the Harvard Business School," book review by Andrew Tobias, a contributing editor of *New York* magazine. *Fortune.* 88:179-80. D. '73. Reprinted by permission.

do what they do because they are resigned to it. Those who do what they do because they enjoy it. And those who do what they do in order to get to the next rung up the ladder, and from there to the next, and the next, and the next.

The fifteen hundred or so M.B.A. [Master of Business Administration] candidates at Harvard Business School fall mostly into that third group. Certainly students do not go to Harvard Business School, as they might to Harvard College, for the experience, or for learning's own sake. Nor are many of them, after they graduate, likely to do what they do for *its* own sake. Most are likely to be doing it in order to get to do something else. This is not surprising—Harvard's first criterion in selecting M.B.A. candidates is motivation. And because of their high degree of motivation, their native ability, their Harvard training, Harvard label, Harvard contacts, and Harvard-bred self-confidence—not necessarily in that order—Harvard M.B.A.'s do indeed seem to climb from rung to rung like rhesus monkeys.

Who are these people? How does the admissions office of Harvard Business School go about issuing its tickets to the top? And once a class is selected, what magic does Harvard perform in two years to justify the formidable—some say inflated—reputation of "the Harvard M.B.A."? Is the education really so outstanding? If so, just what do the students learn?

An Impassioned Indictment

Answers to some of these questions are to be found in *The Gospel According to the Harvard Business School . . .* by Peter Cohen, who received an M.B.A. from Harvard in 1970. The book is not, as its title might suggest, a summary of the management methods and other wisdom with which the Business School imbues its students. It is not any sort of management textbook, or even an *Up the Organization* [the popular 1970 work by Robert Townsend], full of pithy (though dubious) management tenets.

What is it, then? Two things. It is a rather good, if long-winded, description of what goes on at Harvard Business School—the students and faculty, the case method, the buzz words, the work load, the competitive pressure. And it is an impassioned, but unpersuasive, indictment of the "cut-throat" atmosphere the B-School fosters—an atmosphere that the author sees as pervading the American educational and economic systems. The indictment is strikingly similar to that leveled against Harvard Law School by the . . . movie *The Paper Chase*. Cohen, who is Swiss and a graduate of Princeton, calls for greater reliance on cooperation in American society, and less on competition.

In diary form, Cohen takes the reader through two years, 1968-70, that were for him and his ninety-three section-mates sometimes exhausting ("Kandel almost fell out of his chair, yawning"), sometimes painful (you could "hear the terror of being rebuked" in a student's voice), and sometimes tragic ("On this day, a perfect spring day, David Rosen shot himself in his office"). In the process, he brings the somewhat-more-than-human whiz-kid image of the Harvard M.B.A. into a truer perspective. "Even at the Business School," he writes, "there are a good many quite ordinary people." But, he adds, "they are ordinary people making an extraordinary effort, which is kind of extraordinary in itself." Indeed, a good case could be made that students at Harvard Business School—on average, with lots of exceptions—are not as bright as students throughout the rest of the university. At least in part, this may reflect the degree to which raw intelligence is less important, and qualities of leadership more important, for the corporate manager than for the corporate lawyer, the nuclear physicist, or the philosopher.

Distilled Common Sense

Cohen has a knack for characterization. Though the students and teachers he sketches are partially disguised, B-School alumni will readily recognize some of them, as individuals or as types. In addition, Cohen describes enough of the course material and recreates enough classroom discussions to give the reader a sense of the "case method," and how it works (when it works). Harvard does not teach business facts, or even rules of thumb. Instead, it attempts to teach students how to look at problems. As one of Cohen's classmates puts it: "Really, the content of what the Business School has to offer is just distilled common sense."

Harvard M.B.A.'s are not expected to know the costs-per-thousand of different media, but to understand broad marketing strategies. Columbia M.B.A.'s can be hired to work out the actual media schedule—or so the thinking goes, though it is seldom expressed quite that way. The Harvard M.B.A. learns enough to know what a regression analysis is, and when it may be useful. The Chicago M.B.A. learns how to *do* one.

This general-management orientation, which provides Harvard M.B.A.'s with a broad perspective, if not much humility, prompted Robert Townsend to counsel in *Up the Organization*: "Don't hire Harvard Business School graduates. [They are trained] for only three posts—executive vice president, president, and board chairman." Notice that Townsend suggests Harvard M.B.A.'s make lousy employees, not that they make lousy executive vice presidents, presidents, or board chairmen.

Cohen credits the B-School with considerable success in teaching common sense. Indeed, he perceives in the classroom give-and-take a certain human drama that others may have missed (or even dozed through), as when he writes:

The professor's question hits you like a brilliant light, with a sharp pain that cuts you loose, plunging you into a silence of faint, garbled sounds like recording tape run backward, sending you tumbling through this crazy, windowless room, head over heels, head over heels.

But the common sense Harvard teaches, Cohen feels, is taught at intolerable psychic expense. While he was there, one of his professors and two fellow M.B.A. candidates killed themselves.

During those years, the students of Harvard University were often in a state of turmoil. But B-School students, at least in Cohen's eyes, failed to show much concern. During the student disorders instigated by the SDS [Students for a Democratic Society] in the spring of 1969, the B-School faculty—who tend to be more liberal than their students—suspended classes so students could attend a universitywide debate over whether or not to strike. Most M.B.A. candidates took to the tennis courts or the computer room instead. "All this time, while ten thousand people across the street [in Harvard stadium] were wondering what their world was coming to, the staff of Corporation 7 [a student-run mock corporation in a computer-simulated business game] was busy figuring out ways to increase their profit."

"To Live in Crowded Isolation"

Cohen sees the inhumanity of the times reflected in the American educational process, epitomized by the Harvard Business School.

You learn in school not to . . . [care] if the people you climb over are weak or sick or small or blind. You understand that everybody is your enemy, and you learn to fear and hate people, to live in crowded isolation for the rest of your days. But above all, you learn never to show your weaknesses and to put up a front at all times, and you learn to hate yourself for doing it.

No doubt there are elements of truth in that indictment, however exaggerated. And one must understand that it was written in the context of the tragic suicide of a twenty-two-year-old M.B.A. candidate. Cohen clearly feels that the competitive pressure of the B-School had a lot to do with this suicide (and the other two as well). "The Business School has become accomplice to another death," he writes. "The cost of our education is going up." But the case ultimately makes no sense: the student had *finished* his two-year ordeal, if that is what it was, had done well, and had lined up a job with McKinsey, the prestigious consulting firm. So how does his suicide corroborate Cohen's argument?

The answer to Cohen's criticism of the B-School's pressure-cooker atmosphere may be that the heat should be turned down somewhat, which in fact has happened in the three and a half years since Cohen was there. Or it may be that this was not the right school for him. "Cohen," according to one of his former professors, "was one of the few true poets to come through this place—a member of the Swiss upper class, with very little quantitative ability, who really wanted to be a writer."

AN OMBUDSMAN FOR EXECUTIVES? [2]

In a recent Supreme Court decision on pornography, Justice Potter Stewart stated that although he did not know how to define it, he knew it when he saw it.

Much the same can be said about justice. It is a widely cherished value, but difficult to define. Yet people can sense whether justice is done; and they can get passionate about an injustice, particularly when they are its victims.

Consider the following:

Frank L. had been the marketing vice president of his company's products division for two years. He was energetic, imaginative, well-liked and successful. However he incurred the displeasure of a senior vice president who decided that he ought to be replaced with a man of his own choosing and previously unknown to the company.

One Monday morning Frank L. was advised that in a week another man would be the marketing vice president. He had received no previous warning of any such move, nor had he been given any reason to believe that there was dissatisfaction with his performance.

Outrageous? Indeed! Unusual? Possibly. However, it may not be as uncommon as we should like to think. In higher management, there is a presumption that personal problems

[2] From article by William M. Evan, professor of sociology and management at the Wharton School of the University of Pennsylvania. New York *Times*. p F 12. Ag. 26, '73. © 1973 by The New York Times Company. Reprinted by permission.

are handled in a genteel fashion and that, generally speaking, justice is done. But what happens when an injustice does occur? Why did Frank L. have no way of redressing the wrong? Why did he not have the right of "due process" routinely accorded to any union members?

If Frank L. had been a unionized assembly-line worker, his foreman could not have arbitrarily dismissed him without violating the collective-bargaining agreement and triggering a grievance case.

Is unionization of managers the answer? Perhaps, but this is no more likely to occur in the near future in the United States, than is substantial unionization of engineers, scientists or other white-collar workers. But what about a corporate ombudsman?

In recent years there has been a tidal wave of proposals to appoint ombudsmen in schools, colleges, churches, hospitals, governmental agencies and city governments.

The Swedish word "ombudsman," meaning an attorney or representative, has been added to English and many other languages. Sweden instituted an ombudsman in 1809. Appointed for four years by a board elected by the parliament, he is responsible only to parliament to which he presents an annual report of his office's activities.

As an officer of parliament he must insure that civil servants properly carry out their administrative duties and protect the citizenry against the bureaucracy's impropriety and insensitivity. This is especially important in industrialized countries where civil servants exercise an increasing influence on the lives of ordinary citizens, through marriage licenses, automobile licenses and social security payments for example.

In addition to investigating alleged maladministration by civil servants, the ombudsman may persuade the government to rectify injustices. The very fact that the ombudsman's office exists, says the Swedish ombudsman, Nils Andren, "provides a constant and healthy influence on the manner in which public servants exercise their duties."

In recent years this Swedish innovation has been exported to many countries, including the United States. The American corporation, however, has yet to adopt it to protect the executive against capricious and unjust treatment.

There are several arguments against the corporation's adopting this Swedish innovation. First, there is a question as to whether the need for an ombudsman is real. Short of a systematic, confidential survey of executives in a national sample of corporations, there is no way to settle this issue to the satisfaction of the doubting Thomases.

From what social scientists have learned about all kinds of organizations, including corporations, however, we should expect to find numerous conflicts at all levels in the managerial hierarchy. These often pave the way for injustice.

Second, some might say, even if a corporation did appoint an ombudsman for executives, no worthwhile executive would avail himself of the ombudsman's services. If he did, so the argument runs, he would be admitting that he has neither the wit nor the imagination to manage his own affairs, let alone those of subordinates.

Third, there is a fairly strong belief in the managerial principles of unity of command and the chain of command. Having recourse to an ombudsman is, in effect, a violation of these principles.

Finally, there is the question of the source and nature of the corporate ombudsman's authority. Would he be the agent of the president or top management, a staff official charged with uncovering and resolving disputes? Would dependence on the president or top management undermine his effectiveness? Or is it likely that a corporation would consent to an independent ombudsman with authority? Should it? If he were independent and without authority, how effective could he be in resolving corporate conflicts?

Since World War II American industry has had an increasing influx of managers with technical expertise, sophistication and sometimes, advanced degrees.

They have been recruited in response to the increasing

complexity of the technology, market structure and political and economic climates in which companies operate both domestically and worldwide. Under such conditions, it is reasonable to expect managers, especially those responsible for different functions, to have honest differences of opinions.

When errors or failures occur, executives, like other mortals, tend to justify their own behavior and look elsewhere for deficiencies and scapegoats. Conflicts thus multiply and go unchecked, and when the participants may impose a resolution, there is a good chance of injustice's being done.

These are but several factors that may encourage corporations to experiment with the Swedish ombudsman model for handling conflicts and insuring justice.

In . . . [a 1971 book, *Organizational Experiments*], I . . . urged executives to view managerial decisions from an experimental perspective. It is easy to lose sight of the fact that the corporation, as a social invention of modern times, is an extraordinarily dynamic institution.

Before this century ends, the corporation will probably be further transformed in an effort to adapt to the volatile environment at home and abroad. The introduction of an ombudsman for executives could enhance the corporation's adaptive and innovative capacity.

THE ROLE OF OUTSIDE DIRECTORS [3]

More than three dozen suits have been filed by disgruntled shareholders of the Penn Central Transportation Company against the members of its board of directors who served prior to its receivership. These suits are based on the rule of law imposing the ultimate legal responsibility for the management of a corporate enterprise upon its board of directors.

[3] Reprint of "Debate on Outside Directors," by Arthur J. Goldberg, former associate justice of the United States Supreme Court and presently in the private practice of law. New York *Times*. p F 1+. O. 29, '72. © 1972 by The New York Times Company. Reprinted by permission.

Yet, the question arises, in light of the complexity of the operation of any large company, of how even the most conscientious outside board members can meet their basic duty of serving responsibly as directors. In addition to this legal obligation, the modern board of directors is properly being called upon to meet the economic and social challenges of the society at large.

The major problem in the corporate director system is the gap between what the law decrees to be the governing role of the corporate director and the reality of management control of the corporation.

Contrary to legal theory, the boards of directors of most of our larger companies do not in fact control and manage their companies, nor are they equipped to do so. Instead, the management hired by the board, presumably to execute decisions of the board, in fact generally decides the course of operations and periodically requests the board to confirm the determinations of the management.

Thus, the board is relegated to an advisory and legitimizing function that is substantially different from the role of policy maker and guardian of shareholder and public interest contemplated by the law of corporations.

At the very best, outside directors of almost all large corporate enterprises under the present system cannot acquire more than a smattering of knowledge about any large and far-flung company of which they are directors. As a result, outside directors often are even unable to ask discerning questions when presented with a complex management decision for approval at the board meetings.

This can result in the outside director not fulfilling his fiduciary responsibility to the shareholders. As one former Penn Central director frankly admitted: "I don't think anybody was aware that it was that close to collapse."

The implication of the Penn Central fiasco for the future of the current director system is that outside directors must ponder how best to reassert the managerial and policy-making functions of the board. A board of directors not aware of recent legal and related developments is not fulfilling its legal and public responsibilities and is only asking for trouble.

While many companies carry liability insurance for their officers and directors, and bylaws often have provisions allowing for indemnification, money can never adequately compensate for the damage done to the reputation of outside directors of personal and professional integrity. Indeed, the $10 million policy purchased in 1968 for Penn Central may be cancelled because of information allegedly concealed when the policy was written.

Factors that may be deemed as illustrative of negligence or mismanagement on the part of directors include:

Ignoring signs of mismanagement and failing to take affirmative action after learning facts sufficient to put a prudent man on notice of possible mismanagement.

Disregard of duties by indifference to responsibilities.

Acting as figureheads with no genuine attempt to oversee the administration of corporate affairs.

Failure to examine and review carefully the books and records of the corporation and management's major policy decisions.

The lack of adequate and persistent investigation by a board of directors of areas of decision such as product-line development, consumer relations, ecology and social issues within the corporate structure can properly lead to charges of corporate irresponsibility against the board itself as well as the corporation as a whole.

As commentators have noted, a corporation with tens of millions of dollars in sales is no longer merely a business with private goals, but is also a social institution with resulting responsibilities. Indeed, everyone has the right to be concerned with the effect of a company's products or practices if they are dangerous, harmful or deceptive in any way.

The dilemma of the corporate director and indeed of the corporation as a whole is how to meet these responsibilities to the shareholders, to the enterprise of the corporation and to the public at large.

It is difficult, if not impossible, under the present director system for the most dedicated director to have much impact on policy decisions. The outside director is simply unable to gather enough independent information to act as a watchdog or sometimes even to ask good questions.

When presented with the agenda of the board meeting, the director is not basically equipped to provide any serious input into the decision. Realistically, it has already been made by management. This mode of operation, however, leaves the director open to justifiable criticism and legal recriminations.

It would be the counsel of wisdom and in the interest of shareholders and the public to provide outside directors with the means whereby they could discharge their fiduciary responsibilities in the conduct of corporate affairs.

To assure that the board of directors of a typical large company is performing its duties by using its best and independent judgment in the interest of the stockholders and the public at large, one of the possible solutions is for the board to establish a committee of overseers of outside directors (the exact name is not important, but the function is).

Such a committee would be generally responsible for supervising company operations on a broad scale and make periodic reports to the board.

To perform these duties adequately this committee would need authorization to hire a small staff of experts who would be responsible only to the board and would be totally independent of management control. In addition, the committee should also be empowered to engage the services of consultants of the highest competence.

As the eyes and ears of the directors, these independent experts and their staff assistants and consultants would look into major policy questions and report to the committee and through them to the board as a whole before decisions are taken on management recommendations.

The fundamental responsibility of these experts, staff and consultants would be to provide an independent source of expertise for the board. This would help enable the board members to fulfill the due diligence requirements of a reasonable independent investigation of company operations.

In addition, it would reassert the position of the board as a focal point for creative policy input for corporate decisions.

The experts, staff assistants and consultants would in turn have to be assured of full and complete cooperation from management and from lower-level corporate employees in filling requests for information. This right to information, of course, is one of the rights as well as a responsibility of corporate directors.

The membership of this group of expert advisers should include representatives from widely divergent areas of expertise.

For technical aspects of product-line development, scientific advisers should be recruited. For a look at future markets and the desires of the public, a demographic expert and consumer adviser should be consulted. To ensure compliance with truth-in-advertising standards, an outside advertising consultant might be utilized.

Other possible experts might include an independent auditor to assure the soundness of the accounting techniques used by the corporation and a disinterested independent financier (for example, a retired executive of an investment banking house) to ascertain whether the operations are being frugally financed.

Finally, some employee representatives might be consulted for their independent view of the performance of the corporation from their perspective. Permanent staff assistants to the overseer committee could perform most of the investigative work necessary for the use of the experts.

The advantages of such a committee and staff of experts are numerous. The most fundamental one is to assure that, as the law demands, the board of directors is managing the corporation in the interest of the shareholder and the public.

It could assure an independent source of creativity. It could be a check and balance on management decisions. Finally, it would help guarantee that the corporation is truly serving the public interest as well as making money for its shareholders.

And I suspect that by informed and independent advice it could help make corporations both more profitable and responsible.

WOMEN IN MANAGEMENT [4]

With a crisp manner and hearty handshake, the ambitious businesswoman often courts success by acting like a man. As one has explained, when she was in her mid-twenties and determined to get ahead at the office, she took her femininity and "stored it away for future consideration." Up to a point, perhaps to middle-management levels, this tactic may prove effective. But to reach the highest levels of business, a woman must clearly and comfortably accept the fact that she is a woman, according to two alumnae of the Harvard Graduate School of Business Administration: Margaret Hennig, thirty-three, and Anne Jardim, thirty-seven. They are so convinced that women must take their own route to the executive suite that they have set up at Simmons College in Boston the nation's first graduate program in management at a woman's school. Beginning . . . [in September 1974], they will train some of the female executives needed as a result of recent legal assaults on sex discrimination in business. (Although 40 percent of the

[4] Reprint of "Madam Executive." *Time*. 103:76-7. F. 18. '74. Reprinted by permission from *Time*, The Weekly Newsmagazine; Copyright Time Inc.

work force is female, less than 2 percent of managers earning over $25,000 per year are women.)

The shortage of women managers is only partly due to discrimination, Hennig and Jardim believe. On the basis of their experience as consultants to such corporations as New England Bell Telephone & Telegraph and the Columbia Broadcasting System, they have discovered that women are held back partly by their own passivity, partly by a vicious circle of misunderstandings. Men tend to assume that women are more interested in marriage or their children than in careers. Women, on the other hand, assume that they will be tolerated only if they are superefficient. So they become experts at one particular job, then hesitate to venture out into something better but more risky. By thus hanging back, they confirm the assumption that they are not really committed to a career.

Moreover, even if they feel they could easily take on more responsibilities, women tend not to demand them, as men often do, but hope to be invited to accept them. Using a dancing school analogy, Hennig notes that women in business management "are all dolled up against the wall, waiting to be chosen."

One female bank vice president, for example, served as acting president for several months, yet was not considered permanently for the job simply because of her sex. She also suspected that her salary was lower than that paid to male vice presidents. Bitterly, she accepted these inequities for years till she consulted with Hennig and Jardim. They told her to add up her assets and make a case for herself. "That was a blinding insight to her," notes Jardim. "My God," responded her boss when the woman finally mustered the courage to show him that she was managing some $25 million in loans, whereas her four male bank colleagues together were handling only $10 million. Shortly afterward, she got a big raise.

Fearing to move upward into an unknown job where they might make mistakes and appear incompetent, resentful women hang back and grow more resentful with the years; they are often seen by other employees, notes Jardim, as "business bitches." Unlike their male coworkers, women have no "support system," revolving around the lunch hour and the locker room, where men share valuable business tips about moving up the ladder. Excluded from the male system, women must establish their own.

Some of Hennig's notions stem in part from her 1970 Ph.D. thesis, expanded with the help of Jardim, . . . [to] be published . . . under the title *Women Executives: Pioneers in Management*. For the thesis, Hennig interviewed twenty-five top female executives to discover what characteristics they shared. All of them had in effect shelved their femininity for many years in favor of their jobs. But when they reached the middle-management stage of their careers, usually in their late thirties or early forties, they all, in various ways, declared a moratorium on their blind striving for success. They began to devote more time to their personal lives. Some married, some did not; but all, in Hennig's words, "signified their willingness to be viewed as women." After a period of reassessment they managed, for the first time, to blend their femininity with their careers. Their relationships at work became more open and effective, and it was then that they made the final leap upward to become presidents or vice presidents of their firms.

A similar group of women whom Hennig studied, by continuing through their forties to act as much like men as possible, remained in the levels of middle management and were "closed, bitter, defensive, unhappy." Exactly why one group reexamined and redirected their lives while the other did not remains a question. But Hennig's and Jardim's advice to the woman who wants a successful career in business is unequivocal: don't be a wallflower, don't fear failure, and above all, be your womanly self.

BLACK DIRECTORSHIPS [5]

Mr. Speaker, the September 1973 issue of *Black Enterprise* published an article by Lester Carson concerning black directors on major corporate boards. The article describes the roles of the black men and women who sit on the boards of major US corporations. The existence of these black directors shows evidence of a slow but steady increase in excellent directorship opportunities for blacks throughout America. Ten years ago there were no black directors—now there are seventy-two, throughout the United States.

Eleven of these directors, I am proud to say, are from my own district of Washington, D.C., and I believe that these upstanding men and women are worthy of mention in this House. They are as follows: Tyrone Brown, director, Post-Newsweek Stations, Inc.; Clifford Alexander, Jr., director, Dreyfus Third Century Fund, Octagon Industries Inc., Pennsylvania Power & Light Company; James E. Cheek, director, First National Bank of Washington; Charles T. Duncan, director, National Bank of Washington; Cleveland L. Dennard, director, Chesapeake & Potomac Telephone Company; Theodore R. Hagans, Jr., director, Potomac Electric Power Company; William S. Harps, director, National Bank of Washington, Perpetual Building Savings & Loan Association; Patricia R. Harris, director, Chase Manhattan Bank, International Business Machines Corporation, National Bank of Washington, Scott Paper Company; Belford Lawson Jr., director, Chesapeake & Potomac Telephone Company; William Lucy, director, National Bank of Washington; and Hobart Taylor, Jr., director, Aetna Life & Casualty, Great Atlantic and Pacific Tea Company, Standard Oil Company, Westinghouse Electric Corporation.

The article by Lester Carson describes the influence of

[5] From extension of remarks by Walter E. Fauntroy (Democrat, Delegate, District of Columbia), October 15, 1973. *Congressional Record.* (daily ed.) 120:E6492-3. O. 15, '73.

these people along with the other sixty-one black directors in America. It illustrates their influence on their respective boards as well as how they represent the black community. The reasons for the emergence of black directors vary. Their own sharply contrasting views of why they were chosen and what is expected of them as directors show evidence of this. There are some who consider themselves black directors and others who say they are directors who just happen to be black. All of these people, however, serve as spokesmen for the black community, whether they realize it or not. Company policy, as it affects black people, can now be represented in the executive office where action can take place to alleviate problems affecting black labor. The sophistication of their position does not excuse the black director from the role of representative in the front office and this is fully realized and accepted by most black directors.

It is important to note, that these black directors are chosen for the skills which they offer to the company, and not simply because they are black. Their role as representative of the black people never exceeds their role as director but neither is it suppressed. These directors have beneficial suggestions which they offer to their boards which often benefit the black people. The article above mentioned gives a very good illustration of this. Carson writes:

In New York City, home mortgages in slum areas traditionally have been difficult to obtain. In recent years, though, the First National City Bank has stopped "redlining" slum areas, and in addition has helped Bedford-Stuyvesant Restoration Corporation establish a $64 million home mortgage pool. Restoration president Franklin A. Thomas, a director of Citibank, says his presence conceivably hastened the change in bank policy. "It's clear to me," he says, "that the bank's sensitivity to areas like Bedford-Stuyvesant and Harlem is increased by the presence of someone who is of, from, and associated with these areas and knows a little something about how banks can help or hurt development processes in these areas. Maybe it would have happened anyway," Thomas concedes, "but one measure of your success as a director is that the things of concern to you as a black person become of concern to the board and the company."

I sincerely hope that the number of black directors on the major corporate boards continues to increase, thereby improving the black community's representation in management and opening new doors to better opportunities for promising black executives and businessmen.

SUPPORT FOR EMPLOYEE-CRITICS [6]

If you're convinced your boss is putting out an unsafe product or wasting taxpayer money through mismanagement, can you speak up candidly without losing your job?

Rarely, according to the case studies of those who have dared.

However, slowly but steadily the situation is improving, say researchers at Ralph Nader's Clearinghouse for Professional Responsibility. Apparently legal protection and colleague support for those who do blow the whistle on government or industry in the name of the public interest is coming.

One well-publicized case which recently took a turn that is proving inspiring to many who have been reticent to speak their piece is that of A. Ernest Fitzgerald.

He is the former civilian cost analyst for the Air Force who, calmly and accurately, predicted in testimony on Capitol Hill . . . [in 1969] that the cost overrun on the C5A would amount to more than $2 billion.

Shortly afterward, he was dismissed from his $36,000 a year job, though ostensibly not for political reasons.

After a lengthy and costly legal fight, financed in large part by the American Civil Liberties Union, which took an interest in the case, Mr. Fitzgerald . . . [in 1973] was ordered reinstated to a position with the Air Force and deemed eligible to collect back pay.

One of those extremely pleased by this turn of events—

[6] Reprint of "Help for Workers Who Blow the Whistle on Employers," article by Lucia Mouat, staff correspondent. *Christian Science Monitor.* p 22. N. 19, '73. Reprint by permission from *The Christian Science Monitor.* © 1973 The Christian Science Publishing Society. All rights reserved.

"I'm very happy for Ernie, he's an outstanding American" —is Henry Durham of Marietta, Georgia, another whistle-blower whose experience was a particularly difficult one.

Mr. Durham was a former production control supervisor at Lockheed Aircraft's Marietta plant. When he witnessed what he calls "gross mismanagement," including what he charged was falsification of company records to trigger certain installment payments due the company, he took his complaint through the industry ranks on up to the president and the chairman of the board. The responsiveness, he says, was nil.

Eventually he left the company, and, still concerned, spelled out the problem publicly before a congressional committee. A General Accounting Office report, researched shortly afterward, confirmed the substance of his findings.

All this has taken a heavy toll on Mr. Durham and his family. "I've lost almost everything I had fighting this thing," he admitted in a telephone interview with the *Monitor* from Florida where he is still, three years after the event, looking for work.

He came close to taking one job, but the board of directors of the firm said the "repercussions from Lockheed" would be too great for them to take him on.

At one point during his whistle-blowing experience, he was receiving so many threatening phone calls that he and his family asked for protection of Federal marshals, who subsequently set up house in the Durhams' home for two months.

However, despite all this and the fact that he has still not found a satisfactory job after nineteen years of work for Lockheed, he says of his whistle-blowing action: "I'd do it a thousand times over, despite the hardships. . . . I have a strong feeling that it's more patriotic to do something about things that are wrong, even though it may rock the boat, than to sit back and do nothing."

The impact of Mr. Durham's action on Lockheed?

"Nothing has changed," he says. "They've lost a lot of work. The C5A contract is gone, of course. People blame me for it."

Mr. Durham says he has had letters from many other company workers around the country equally convinced their speaking out would be in the public interest but who are afraid to because of the job consequences. That's why he stresses the need for more legislative safeguards to protect such employees.

Current laws protecting government employees are stronger than those aiding workers in private industry. An employee in the public sector, says Fritzie Cohen of Mr. Nader's Clearinghouse, is at least entitled to a day in court —if he has the money to support the fight.

"In private industry, if your employer doesn't like your politics, he can fire you," says Mrs. Cohen. "You lose certain constitutional rights when you take the job."

Currently on the books are provisions in the Occupational Safety and Health Act and the Water Pollution Control Act which afford some protection for workers who report violations of those laws. However, Clearinghouse workers consider the present path of recourse—to seek reinstatement via the Labor Department—unsatisfactory, since the government agency could conceivably choose to do nothing.

Some Potential Support

Certainly an important potential prod for stronger legislation and a rich possible source of moral support for the blue-collar or professional whistle-blower is the union or the association to which the employee may belong.

Unfortunately unions have traditionally been reluctant to wade into this muddy-water area and, indeed, many collective bargaining agreements specifically label the product of a company as management's concern.

To date, professional associations have not been much more progressive in supporting the professional and public responsibilities of their members, either. Currently far ahead of the others is the American Chemical Society, which recently elected as president a candidate who had strongly made known his concerns in this area. That group, some 110,000 members strong, is in the process of setting up a legal defense fund to help those fighting job dismissals where the society deems a fight justified.

Also, Chemical Society members have drafted and are backing an employee bill of rights amendment to the National Labor Relations Act.

Peter Petkas, of the Clearinghouse, hopes the example may spur other associations to follow suit. He puts the situation bluntly: "If professional societies or unions, or both, don't do anything, nothing will ever be done."

Criticism Often Difficult

One reason why associations have been slow to move is that sometimes a whistle-blowing criticism reflects directly on other members of the group. Such was the case with the California Society of Professional Engineers and three local chapter members who were critical of the safety features of the engineering design of the Bay Area Rapid Transit (BART) System.

After putting their case to a BART board member who mentioned it at a public meeting, the three were fired. In effect, they had been criticizing the work of consulting engineers, a category of the profession which happened to be in the influential leadership position of the state association.

Ray Anderson, a man who headed the state society's investigation of the three engineers' charges, and who is now working in Washington, says the organization's words were originally supportive of the three, "but the actions were something else." In short, the men, now suing BART for damages stemming from their dismissal, were largely on their own.

"A lot of engineers just don't understand the code of ethics of the profession," says Mr. Anderson. "Their first priority is commitment to the public interest . . . that's what

Watergate is all about. Who do you owe your prime allegiance to—your supervisor or the people?"

Certainly, there are careful lines to be drawn.

Mr. Petkas, whose small Clearinghouse group advises
many would-be whistle-blowers on whether or not and how
to proceed, stresses that all are urged to first exhaust all possible channels *within* their organizations. Each of the eleven
cases listed in the group's book *Whistle Blowing—Profiles
in Conscience and Courage* affirms that the public disclosure
route was taken only as a last resort.

Also, an employee's motivation is sometimes mixed, and
he may not have the facts to back up his contention. "We've
certainly discouraged a lot more whistle-blowers than we've
encouraged," says Mr. Petkas.

THE WORK AND THE WORKER [7]

Not long ago a management expert visited the typewriter
assembly plant operated . . . [in Amsterdam] by International Business Machines and denounced the plant's new
production techniques as "communism." He was followed
by another outside expert, who looked over the plant and
declared with disapproval that it was "producing neocap-
italists."

Both had taken note, from opposite points of view, of
a striking fact, visible at IBM here as well as at other industrial plants in Europe—notably in Sweden, at Volvo,
Saab, Atlantic Copco and other installations. New methods
of production being introduced and developed tend to
"push decision making down" within an industrial organization, reducing the demands on high-level management and
increasing the responsibility of workers on the line.

Thus, the new IBM production system relies on "mini-
lines" which are, in effect, simplified business units making

[7] Reprint of column by Tom Wicker, associate editor. New York *Times*.
p 39. Je. 18, '74. © 1974 by The New York Times Company. Reprinted by
permission.

many of their own decisions on production, engineering, quality control and materials handling. And the firm is pleased enough with the results that it is planning a new parts manufacturing facility here, to be built from scratch on the new production ideas.

The Amsterdam plant has been IBM's primary European typewriter assembly plant since 1961, when it employed 600 people. Production expanded rapidly throughout the sixties, so that by 1969 the plant employed 1,600 people. Fifty thousand typewriters were put together in 1968, a goal of 80,000 was set for 1969, and about 100,000 were foreseen for 1970.

This rapidly expanding production was complicated by customer demands in an export market, with 90 percent of production going to seventy-five different countries. There were eighteen basic typewriter models, each with about two thousand five hundred parts, twenty-five special models, well over a hundred different keyboards and typeheads (the plant can turn out a typewriter with a Thai keyboard and a machine that types from right to left for Iran and Israel).

The IBM plant then relied upon two conventional assembly lines, each nearly two hundred meters long, with about seventy workers on each line. The method of increasing productivity was to lengthen the line, add workers, further simplify the job of each, and reduce the time it took to do it. By 1969, assembly-line workers worked for an average of only three minutes on each typewriter coming down the line. Some felt themselves little more than robots.

The long lines were poorly adapted to the production flexibility IBM required; worse, production quality was low and 12 percent of man-hours went into overtime for the repair of defective machines coming off the line. Thirty percent of the work force left their jobs every year; among the others absenteeism was soaring. Management had grave doubts that production could be sufficiently expanded under such conditions.

A survey disclosed that Dutch workers, particularly

younger persons with higher levels of education than their parents, wanted more responsible jobs, a more sociable working climate, a better relationship to management and to the product—all taking precedence over higher wages and better career opportunities.

Now there are nine "mini-lines," each employing about twenty workers and each producing a complete and recognizable unit. Three months after the completion of the changeover, in August 1971, production had risen by 18 percent (after an initial sag); by December, 1972, production was up by 35 percent and by December, 1973, it had risen by 46 percent.

The new system sharply improved quality and reduced overtime. The mini-lines were easier to adapt to flexible production. Workers felt themselves more involved with a product they saw through to completion, rather than one they worked on for three minutes. Because of this increased responsibility and the longer work cycle, many annoying individual controls previously imposed by management could be abolished. Absenteeism and personnel turnover dropped. Many production decisions—for instance, the best way to incorporate a product change—now are decided on the line by the workers involved. They also decided for themselves to take a vacation period between Christmas and New Year's Day, and sufficiently increased production to make the time off possible.

The old system forced a worker to adapt himself to a set task. The mini-line system adapts the work to be done to the need of the men and women who do it. Both the necessity for such a change, and the benefits to be derived from it, are widely recognized in Europe, and sooner or later will make themselves felt in the United States.

JOBHOLDER MEETINGS:
A CHANCE TO QUESTION MANAGEMENT [8]

"Is there a corporate policy on streaking?" asked one employee.

"Yes," responded P. T. Corbalis, a vice president whose hair was streaked. "If an employee streaks once he receives a reprimand. Twice, he receives a written reprimand. The third time, he's terminated. The policy is called three streaks and you're out," he said.

"What about the possibility of assigning parking spots . . . ?" another employee asked.

"We've talked about it, but it's a very difficult job," responded Fred A. Grosebeck, vice president of operations. "If somebody gets assigned a spot in the back of the lot, they're not going to like it, and what do you do if somebody dies, reassign all the spots?"

Typical Questions

These are just samples of the kinds of questions and answers that are likely to be voiced at an annual jobholder meeting such as the one held here today by the management of Pitney-Bowes, Inc., the nation's largest manufacturer of postal meters and mailing equipment.

Yesterday's two-hour session was one of eighteen such meetings to be held this year by the corporation, which has held them annually for twenty-eight years. It will take all eighteen meetings for management to reach its more than twelve thousand employees throughout the United States.

Employees and top management generally agree that the meetings are essential in the company's overall approach to good in-house relations.

Humor is not a result of every topic of discussion at these jobholder meetings. They are held to allow employees

[8] From "Jobholders Get Chance to Air Gripes at Pitney-Bowes," by Reginald Stuart, staff reporter. New York *Times*. p 43. Ap. 12, '74. © 1974 by the New York Times Company. Reprinted by permission.

and management to discuss what employees really have on their minds. Subjects include higher wages, pension benefits, the future of the company, in which many of them hold stock, as well as working conditions and safety.

"Last year was a difficult year, and there is no way for us to ignore the damage," said Fred T. Allen, president and chairman of the board of Pitney-Bowes. "We are determined that 1974 will be a good year and believe me we need it," he told the employees, dressed in their regular work clothes during their regular working time. Mr. Allen, who has worked for Pitney-Bowes since 1938, acknowledged that his employees knew a lot about the operations of the company and that last year's $37 million writeoff and subsequent decision to pay no dividends was not some corporate business that never got into the production rooms. He advised them that increased wages, incentives and dividends hinged on increased productivity.

After the showing of a brief film called "Special Responsibility," a film about Pitney-Bowes, the meeting turned to the airing of compliments and criticisms by jobholders, and the questions flowed for more than an hour.

In addition to the audience of several hundred manufacturing section employees, there were seven management representatives . . . who responded to many of the questions. In addition, the Council of Personnel Relations, elected representatives of the employees in various divisions of the company, had nine representatives seated opposite the management team.

Among the more serious concerns of some jobholders was the question of pension benefits. Why can't employees who have thirty years of service and retire get full benefits even if they aren't sixty-five?

Expense Is Cited

Mr. Allen answered that the company could not afford to pay full benefits to an employee who at age fifty, for example, had accumulated thirty years service and had retired.

They could get the full pension benefits at sixty-five but only partial ones until then.

The employees' questions, as important to them as the questions a board member would ask at an annual board meeting, were read by employee representatives, in cases where an employee wanted to remain anonymous.

On some occasions, however, they came from the floor. One such query concerned how hot it must get in a particular work section before employees are allowed to go home. The question was raised because the section became so hot last summer that some employees left. The answer was 100 degrees. The audience groaned. Management agreed to reassess the situation.

The employees had the questions although management did not always have satisfactory answers. But employees at the Pitney-Bowes plant as well as management representatives characterized these annual meetings as healthy endeavors.

One employee, who had worked for the company for twenty years, pointed out, however, that these meetings would lose their legitimacy if Mr. Allen, or whoever was the boss, failed to show up. "You get straight answers when the top management people are here," the employee said, "whereas with management people you don't get much done."

V. THE MULTINATIONALS

EDITOR'S INTRODUCTION

The multinational is the most written- and talked-about corporate development since President Theodore Roosevelt attempted to break up the trusts. Many of the criticisms and defenses of these corporate giants are similar to those affecting corporations in general. The potential for good or harm is simply multiplied in corporations that live under many flags.

First, a *U.S. News and World Report* article outlines the magnitude of the question, particularly with regard to American firms operating abroad. Then a selection from *Newsweek* examines in depth the problems of one multinational, explaining how it must be run for the benefit of all countries in which it operates, as well as sow the seeds for profit. It is a tightrope affair from country to country but with stakes worth the risk, despite expropriation in countries like Chile and structural changes in relationships with the oil-rich countries. As noted in these articles, Senator Frank Church of Idaho, chairman of a subcommittee on multinational corporations, has begun an investigation into these matters and has held hearings on International Telephone and Telegraph and the Overseas Private Investment Corporation; the Burke-Hartke bill, and similar bills in the succeeding Congress, have not been enacted into law. In the last selection, Raymond Vernon spells out the complexities of "accountability" and suggests that some binding agreements among nations may be necessary.

The articles in this section do not particularly take into account the oil crisis that began in 1973 or the natural-resources crisis that is looming on the horizon—their effect on multinationals will be a continuing topic of discussion in the days, months, and years ahead.

MULTINATIONALS UNDER FIRE [1]

Reprinted from *U.S. News & World Report*.

Congress, labor unions and foreign nations are aiming increased criticism at the growing economic power of "multinationals"—big US-based companies that also operate overseas.

Pending tax-reform and foreign-trade bills contain proposals that would curb the growth of these firms and require more rapid payment of US taxes on profits earned abroad.

There are about 3,600 American companies that have at least one foreign subsidiary, according to the Department of Commerce.

Only about 200 of these have overseas operations large enough to be considered truly "multinational." But they include some of the heavyweights in American business: General Motors, Mobil, International Business Machines, International Telephone & Telegraph, Western Electric, Rockwell International, United States Steel, Boeing and Du Pont—companies whose names are as well known in many foreign nations as in the US.

Attacks on multinationals range over a wide variety of issues, among them:

Job opportunities in the US are reduced as production facilities and technology are transferred to plants overseas. Organized labor has charged that half a million jobs have been "exported" by US-based multinational corporations.

Profits earned by American-based firms abroad are not taxable in the US until they are returned to this country.

[1] From "Why 'Multinationals' Are Under Fire at Home, Abroad." *U.S. News & World Report*. 74:64-6. My. 21, '73.

Critics say this deferral is in effect an interest-free loan to US subsidiaries overseas which can be manipulated to the advantage of the parent company.

Some foreign nations are becoming sensitive to the presence of US multinationals, calling them a form of American economic imperialism and exploitation. Hostility in some countries has led to demands for an end to further investment by American companies.

Multinationals have been accused of undermining the dollar and trade balance. Some critics suggest that US firms engaged in excessive speculation during the recent dollar devaluations by shifting their funds from weak currencies to strong ones.

Huge Stake

These allegations and others will be raised in congressional debate this year when trade and tax legislation is considered. The stakes riding on the outcome are enormous, especially for business.

The total value of US investment assets abroad, according to the Senate Finance Committee, is about $203 billion, including short-term assets. Manufacturing makes up 38 percent of that total, petroleum 22 percent, and other businesses, such as food producers, banks and communications companies, 40 percent.

Europe has surpassed Canada as the main area for US investments abroad, with Latin America in third place. Annual worldwide sales of foreign manufacturing affiliates of US firms exceed $90 billion, according to congressional sources.

The multinationals are quick to come to their own defense on all charges against them.

For example, the companies deny that they are fleeing high wage rates in the US simply to utilize lower-salaried workers in foreign countries.

This view has gotten some strong support from massive

studies of multinationals recently completed by the United States Tariff Commission, the Department of Commerce and the Emergency Committee for American Trade, a multinational lobby group.

An analysis of the Tariff Commission's data produces this conclusion:

Multinational firms generated $2 billion more in exports than imports, made a positive contribution to the balance of payments, and under the most reasonable assumptions, caused a net increase of half a million jobs in the US during 1966-70, the period covered in the study. Most of the new jobs, however, resulted from operations of foreign multinationals with plants in the US.

Foreign Markets

In fact, labor-cost considerations were secondary in most decisions to invest abroad, the study found. Much more important were the threats of being denied access to foreign markets and the need for control of raw materials.

The Emergency Committee for American Trade (ECAT) survey also indicates that US multinational companies generally tend to be market-oriented rather than cost-oriented.

Only in industries such as electronic assembly, shoes and apparel—in which labor costs make up a very high percentage of total costs—was the need for cheaper labor a major incentive to invest in a foreign country, according to the ECAT survey.

The Tariff Commission pointed out that labor costs abroad average about 65 percent of what multinational firms would pay in the US. Thus, the big multinationals—which incidentally tend to pay higher wage rates in the US than firms without foreign investment—do benefit from savings by hiring workers overseas.

The Commission report also tended to support the charge that American multinationals caused a loss of jobs in the US. Under the most reasonable assumptions, a total of about 1 million new jobs in the US have been created by operations of both US-based and foreign-based multinational firms.

However, only 461,200 of these jobs can be attributed to home operations of US multinationals. And, the Commission estimated, a total of 603,100 potential American jobs were lost during 1966-70 as US operations moved to other countries, thus leaving a net loss of 141,900 jobs attributable to the American companies.

Yet another recent multinational study—this one by the Commerce Department—notes that most of the jobs created in the US by multinational firms were filled by "white collar" managerial, research and service employees, while "blue collar" production-line workers tended to be displaced.

Exports Boosted

The Tariff Commission study challenged a frequent contention that multinational companies contribute to the rising US trade deficit by widening the balance-of-payments gap. In fact, instead of reducing US exports, foreign investment by US firms seems to have stimulated them.

Between 1966 and 1970, US and foreign multinationals had a net beneficial impact of $3.4 billion on the US balance of trade.

Thus, multinationals apparently made a major, positive contribution to the US balance of payments and were not a factor in the deterioration of the trade deficit during the late 1960s.

Foreign countries—as well as the US—benefit from investment by American multinationals, the Tariff Commission found.

Private US investors are among the principal sources of investment capital for underdeveloped nations. Large oil and mining companies have played major roles in tapping the mineral resources in all parts of the world. US investment in manufacturing is also important to many developing countries. Most US investment in manufacturing, however, takes place in countries that are already developed or well along the road to development.

The Big Eight

In 1970, the Tariff Commission said, foreign direct investment in plant and equipment in manufacturing by US firms totaled $6.5 billion—up more than 42 percent from the $4.6 billion spent in 1966. About 64 percent of this amount was invested in 1970 in eight countries: Canada, Great Britain, Belgium, Luxembourg, France, West Germany, Mexico and Brazil.

US investment plays a crucial role in the growth of the eight countries. US-based multinationals in 1970 accounted for 13 percent of all capital spending in those nations, and 22 percent of the capital spending in the industrial "backbone" sectors—metals, machinery and transportation equipment.

The Commission did not comment on the growing European sensitivity to American ownership of manufacturing capacities within the Common Market. However, it did determine that Americans had gained control over important sectors of foreign commerce, largely with the foreigners' own money—a finding that nationalists find particularly galling.

Shifting Funds

Because they have large amounts of capital at their disposal, US multinationals have been accused of precipitating the monetary crises that have shaken the financial world recently.

The Tariff Commission found that private corporations at the end of 1971 controlled approximately $250 billion in short-term liquid assets, with the bulk of that amount—some $190 billion—held by corporations and banks headquartered in the US.

There is widespread agreement that the huge dollar holdings of American corporations and overseas branches of American banks can trigger massive monetary crises. The size of these assets alone does not create a crisis, but the movement of even a small fraction of them out of one currency into another would set off violent tremors throughout the world monetary system.

Because foreign governments generally hold a relatively small amount of capital in convertible short-term assets, any showdown in the international money market between foreign governments and the private sector would find the governments hopelessly outgunned, the Tariff Commission concluded.

Subsequent evaluation of the Tariff Commission figures by officials in the Treasury and Commerce Departments give a less alarming view of the power US multinationals hold in the money market. About $10 billion to $12 billion is readily available in corporate tills on any given day for participation in "hot money" flows, officials say.

Senator Frank Church, an Idaho Democrat, announced May 8 [1973] that the Senate Foreign Relations Subcommittee on Multinational Corporations would survey the largest corporations to determine the extent to which their transactions affected the February dollar devaluation.

Multinationals contend that they seek only to protect themselves from devaluation and do not speculate on currencies. They say they may react to an already existing crisis, but do not seek to cause disruptions.

New World Order?

Some business experts believe that multinational concerns—because of the interlocking agreements they engender between countries—are creating a new world order and an economic basis for national interdependence and peace.

This prospect has been raised by William I. Spencer, president of the First National City Bank, New York, who suggests that interrelated business ventures among nations will impose a spirit of cooperation and will inhibit aggression—thus lessening the probability of war.

"The political boundaries of nation-states are too narrow and constricted to define the scope and sweep of modern business," Mr. Spencer says. These "new globalists," he adds, consider the entire world as a market, and search everywhere for fresh technology, talented people, novel processes, raw materials, ideas and capital.

Multinationals also . . . [drew] support from the Nixon Administration. In his April 10 [1973] trade message, the President said:

American investment abroad . . . has meant more and better jobs for American workers, has improved our balance of trade and our overall balance of payments, and has generally strengthened our economy.

But big forces are lining up for the imminent battle over trade and tax legislation. "What is at issue today," says a Senate Finance Committee review of the Tariff Commission study, "is the degree of freedom that multinationals should have or the extent of regulation that should be imposed on their present operations and future growth."

GLOBAL COMPANIES: TOO BIG TO HANDLE? [2]

It was early in August 1971, and Donald G. Robbins Jr. had managed to remain calm—a remarkable feat in itself for the chief financial officer of a multinational company in the nail-chewing tension that was gripping the world's money markets. When the White House quietly announced that President Nixon would meet with his key economic advisers at Camp David over the mid-August weekend, the unthinkable suddenly seemed possible: the once-mighty dollar, linchpin of the twenty-seven-year-old international monetary system, could well be devalued. And for furrow-browed Don Robbins, in a cheerless office in the New York headquarters

[2] Reprint of article in *Newsweek*. 80:96-8+. N. 20, '72. Copyright Newsweek, Inc. 1972, reprinted by permission.

of the Singer Company, that could mean losses in his corporate accounts measured in the millions. But Singer's world intelligence network had been warning of the danger for weeks, and Robbins had been quietly shifting the company funds out of dollars into safer currencies wherever possible. On August 13 [1971], just two days before Mr. Nixon stunned the world by unhooking the dollar from its gold mooring, Robbins matter-of-factly covered his last short positions by exchanging $20 million for Swiss francs and British sterling.

For Robbins, the operation was strictly a defensive hedge against the vagaries of the currency markets, and the small profit he chalked up was almost incidental. But since his colleagues at the financial controls of four thousand other multinational companies were doing much the same thing in those tense weeks, they were probably the prime force behind the whole currency crisis. "If you want to find all those evil speculators," says James Meigs, economist for Argus Research Corporation in New York, "don't look for them on the Orient Express. They're on the 5:15 to Larchmont."

That episode neatly sums up the growing misgivings about multinational corporations in capitals around the world. Operating casually across national boundaries, the fast-growing giants have mushroomed from total sales of $200 billion in 1960 to $450 billion a year in goods and services—fully 15 percent of the gross world product. In assets, their treasuries often outstrip those of the countries in which they operate. Their maneuvers defy mere national regulation, and their interests don't necessarily coincide with those of any country, not even their base of operations. "The political boundaries of nation-states," says William I. Spencer, president of the ninety-nation First National City Corporation, "are too narrow and constricted to define the scope and sweep of modern business."

The Muscle of Multinationalism

As Spencer and most of his executive-suite colleagues see it, that's all to the good; the "new globalists," in their own view, are the prime agents for economic development, international prosperity and even world peace. "They seek profitable opportunity in addressing themselves not to the demands of the privileged few," Spencer proclaims, "but to the urgent needs of the overwhelming many." But to skeptics whose main concern is the uncontrolled power being accumulated by the multinational companies, the corporate spokesmen are almost naïvely nearsighted. Even though most companies have shown remarkable restraint in using their awesome leverage, says Melville Watkins of the University of Toronto, there have been exceptions—and "no institution is more vulnerable to the charge of authoritarianism."

Several hundred years of multinational muscle-flexing tend to prove that point. Britain's East India Company, perhaps the archetype of the modern multinational, ruled a fifth of the world's population for nearly two and a half centuries. In the 1930s, United Fruit Company (now United Brands) commanded so enormous a presence in Latin America that it could topple governments, control four million acres of land from Cuba to Ecuador and earn the nickname "el pulpo" (the octopus). In Africa, Liberia was once known simply as the Firestone Republic.

Until recently, all that seemed just a relic of the gaudy past. But in the early 1960s, French President Charles de Gaulle raised the first of a series of warning flags at what he saw as a planned takeover of Europe's industry by American companies. De Gaulle, as it turned out, missed the nature of the challenge, which was both subtler and more sweeping than he thought—not a nationalist plot, but the growth of a new and independent force in the world. The global enterprises, after all, included growing numbers of such non-US names as Siemens, Unilever, Imperial Chemical Industries, Philips and Volkswagen, and the fact that mattered most about them was not their national allegiance but their lack of it. As episodes like the currency crisis proliferated, concern over the role of the multinationals has grown. But it took muckraker Jack Anderson, with his charge that International Telephone and Telegraph Corporation had plotted to undermine Chile's President Salvador Allende Gossens, to touch off real waves of concern. "ITT was the catalyst," says Idaho Democrat Frank Church of the Senate Foreign Relations Committee. "What they did in Chile was so brazen, or seemed so brazen, that responsible people could not ignore them."

Battle of Economic Giants

Church himself is leading the US investigators with a $200,000 subcommittee investigation of global companies slated to begin . . . [in 1973]; by one account, every international lawyer in Washington worth his attaché case has been hired by one or another multinational company to prepare for the barrage. But questions are also being asked in Europe. Tentative inquiries have started from Sweden to Italy, the Common Market has taken a sterner attitude toward antitrust violations, and perhaps most important, international unions have begun exploring effective ways to neutralize the power and flexibility of the global employer. The emerging battle, says international legal expert Samuel Pisar, will pit "two gigantic forces: the economic power of the multinationals and the political power of nation-states." Among the issues being raised: How much influence do global corporations exercise on government foreign-policy decisions? Do their operations dislocate national economies? What effect do they have on world trade and currency flows? In short, have multinational corporations simply grown too big to handle without international regulation?

There is no question that the global giants now manage to run their businesses pretty much to their own advantage. It is often possible, for instance, for the US companies to open a new foreign operation as a branch, deducting its initial losses for US tax purposes, and later converting it to a foreign-based subsidiary whose profits are taxed at a lower rate than the 48 percent US maximum. By adroit bookkeeping and pricing of transactions among subsidiaries across national boundaries, profits may be concentrated in the countries where taxes are lowest. Perhaps worse, there have been suggestions that at least a few multinationals have smuggled hard cash into the US to avoid taxes and to make political payoffs.

The loudest objections, however, are coming from US labor unions, which charge that multinational companies are exporting jobs to their foreign subsidiaries with low labor costs, to produce goods that then underprice US-made products. The companies, for their part, argue that their overseas operations actually increase US exports, and there is impartial evidence to back them up. Nonetheless, the AFL-CIO is pushing hard for the protectionist Burke-Hartke bill, introduced in Congress in September 1971. Among other provisions, the bill would repeal the US income-tax credit on payments of foreign income taxes, require stricter guidelines for depreciation on machinery in foreign plants and put an end to tax-free treatment on income from licensing and transferring patents to foreign corporations. It would also permit new quotas on imports and give the President firm new power to regulate the transfer of capital from a company's US headquarters to its foreign subsidiaries. If enacted, multinational executives uniformly agree, the bill would set off a chain reaction of protectionist legislation in other countries, and thus cast the world into a trade war that would make the recriminations of the 1930s pale by comparison. "Burke-Hartke," says multinational businessman Donald P. Kircher, "would bring our international operations to a screeching halt."

As chairman and chief executive officer of the Singer Company, Kircher, fifty-seven, runs a worldwide enterprise that could serve as a model of US-based corporate multinationalism—and to get a close-up view of the global company's role in the world, *Newsweek* reporters have been studying Singer's operations for the past two months. At once obscure and pervasive, flamboyant and phlegmatic, Singer touches the national life of 180 political jurisdictions, girdling the globe with its famous sewing machines, Friden business machines, industrial sewing and knitting equipment, Link aircraft simulators, home furniture and a swarm of other products. Although it ranks only fifty-third among the world's multinational corporations, Singer has been in existence longer than most, and with foreign operations accounting for nearly 40 percent of its $2.1 billion in sales last year, it has achieved almost supranational status. "We regard the entire world as our area of operation," Kircher declares with a faint smile, "at least as far as we are able to do so politically."

Politically, Singer does well indeed. Its century-old record in overseas operations is remarkably free of controversy, and it succeeds far better than most global companies in maintaining a low profile in local operations. In France, for instance, la Compagnie Singer at 27 avenue de l'Opéra blends into the Parisian business landscape as effectively as any native French firm. And a few years back, Queen Elizabeth herself visited Singer's massive home and industrial sewing machine complex at Clydebank, Scotland, only to discover to her dismay that the plant belonged to the Yanks.

The Queen's ignorance seems understandable enough, since the Clydebank factory dates back nearly a century and the company itself to 1850, the year an ill-tempered second-generation German immigrant named Isaac Singer perfected the sewing machine in his Boston shop. Both company and inventor were producing prolifically by 1863—the former at a rate of twenty thousand machines annually, the latter well on his way to twenty-four children by two wives and three known mistresses. And from the early days, the company sought a world role. By 1913, four decades after Isaac Singer retired to baronial splendor in Europe with $13 million, the company had reached annual sales of 3 million machines and controlled fully 70 percent of the world market.

Great Restraint—Sometimes

In most overseas branches, the Singer management was native to the country, and this legacy has done much to preserve the company's solid image abroad. While its larger operations these days are sprinkled with a few Americans, the accent at each unit still has a local flavor. But just as important in preserving relations is the nature of its product mix. Home sewing machines and other consumer products still make up nearly 75 percent of Singer's foreign business, and most countries, especially in less developed areas of the world, look favorably on products that are considered necessities or tend to improve the nation's standard of living. "Singer is neither arrogant nor imperialistic," a Washington-based expert on multinational business told *Newsweek*'s James Bishop Jr. "It goes into the rice fields, for instance, and refrains from attempting to affect the basic structure of the country."

At the New York headquarters, the Singer brass project an almost faceless air of low-key conservatism—an attitude that helps focus real responsibility on local managers around the world. "Too many US companies are strongly managed from New York," says A. C. (Tony) French, a former RAF pilot who heads Singer's British consumer-products subsidiary. "The solution to everything seems to be to send out another American. Singer allows its people to do the job."

But if local operations go sour, Kircher and his coterie of headquarters-based group vice presidents will soon take matters into their own hands. Back in 1967, for example, Singer's International Consumer Products Group—responsible for all consumer products outside the US, Canada and Europe—had overextended credit to customers in South America, Africa and Asia, and delinquent accounts had mounted perilously. Kircher replaced a top layer of management, installed nine executives from New York in key spots on each continent and personally ran the group for nearly two years before gradually releasing it to group vice president Alexander H. Dunbar. Earlier . . . [in 1972], Kircher dispatched Edwin J. Graf, a barrel-chested ex-marine, to the Clydebank factory with orders to settle a costly strike that had dragged on for five weeks. Graf had run Clydebank for eighteen months during the mid-1960s, and in the interim, the Scottish union hierarchy hadn't changed. Within two days of his arrival, he got his old union friends to settle—by giving them pretty much what Singer's local negotiators had refused to provide.

For all its low profile, Singer will do battle with governments themselves when it feels it has been wronged. In Clydebank . . . [in 1972], for instance, it took on the Labour-controlled city council over its refusal to enact Britain's new Housing Finance Act that raises rents on public housing. The council had imposed a property-tax hike to compensate for the funds that higher rents would have produced, and this added some $50,000 to Singer's local tax bill of $540,000. Singer has flatly refused to pay the added revenue, arguing that the council is flouting the law. Similarly, in Turkey, Singer lost its production permit . . . [in October 1972] when it refused to comply with a government order to merge its marketing and manufacturing units so that they would fall under a new, more restrictive law governing profit repatriation.

But such confrontations are rare. Like most multinationals, Singer feels exposed to every breeze of hostile publicity and winces at the hint of controversy; . . . [in August 1972] for instance, the company took some undeserved lumps when a subcontractor used a leased freight car with Singer's name on it in an attempt to smuggle fifty-nine African workers into France. And Singer occasionally bends its capitalistic principles to achieve an entente with its host governments. In Chile, where economic nationalism was blossoming even before Allende came to power, the government of President Eduardo Frei told Singer in the late 1960s to build a manufacturing facility. "We really couldn't justify it economically," recalls Dunbar. "Our product cost would have been twice what we could have imported machines for." But Singer reached a *compromiso*: it agreed to build the plant, but to this day it is used solely as a warehouse—and the company still imports machines.

Connections That Count

Such diplomacy depends largely on good intelligence sources—and while few multinational corporations maintain the mini-State Departments that some international oil companies have in the Middle East, all of them recognize that political and economic nuances in host countries can affect their business. In Singer's case, reports filed regularly to New York from outposts around the world invariably include an appraisal of political conditions. At headquarters, Don Robbins watches world financial markets for subtle shifts in economic policies.

In foreign capitals and business centers, Singer executives mix easily and affably, cultivating government bureaucrats, local banking sources and US embassy staffers. Aristocratic Jacques Ehrsam, for instance, who is president and *directeur général* of La Compagnie Singer in Paris, numbers among his friends Victor Chapot, chief of cabinet in Valéry Giscard d'Estaing's finance ministry; and Austrian-born Robert J. Kendall, the mutton-chopped *Geschäftsführer* of Singer's West German consumer-products subsidiary, keeps in touch with a top government trade official in Frankfurt. But nowhere has this wooing produced a relationship more lucrative than in Brazil, where Singer's sewing-machine operation has become its most profitable subsidiary outside the US.

When Scotsman Alec Dunbar moved into the International Consumer Products Group in 1968, the Brazilian operation controlled more than 60 percent of a market that still showed signs of tremendous growth, but was only breaking even. "We had an uninformed management down there," Dunbar says. "Our guys were hanging out at all the American clubs." But then, through a mutual acquaintance, Dunbar met António Delfim Neto, a former economics professor who is now Brazil's minister of finance and economic affairs. In the next year and a half, Dunbar traveled to Brazil two or three times a month to help pave the way for a modernization program at his plant in Campinas—and almost always, he called on Delfim Neto. The friendship paid off when local opposition blocked Singer's request for duty-free status on $3 million of machinery and equipment it needed to import. After Delfim Neto intervened, the proposal was quickly approved, saving the company $860,000 in import and excise taxes.

Already, exports account for 30 percent of the modernized plant's 300,000-unit annual production, and Singer has begun to ship sewing machines to its marketing groups in places as distant as Singapore, Bangkok and Sydney. But such transactions allow room for considerable intracompany price juggling, and Singer's role as its own supplier has in fact drawn fire from some of its competitors around the world. "Prices fixed for export don't show what I would consider an acceptable return on capital," says a top official of a rival firm in Britain, "and this is bad. Singer is making artificially low profits in high-tax Britain, and it is therefore reducing the amount of foreign currency this country earns."

Covering Assets Abroad

Singer executives argue that their profit-centered operation discourages such hanky-panky by requiring that manufacturing units produce black ink as well as product. But even so, there is room for creative moves in the transfer process. Based on his reading of international monetary markets, Robbins may decide to stretch or contract Singer's normal credit term of ninety days on intracompany settlements, thereby providing purchasing units with a hedge against a possible devaluation or revaluation. And if that isn't enough, he can deal in the "forward" markets—where currencies are traded in much the same way commodities are in the US—to cover an exposed position. . . . [In June 1972], for instance, Robbins had become increasingly concerned with the British pound's obvious weakness. To guard against devaluation, he went to the forward markets and sold short nearly $15 million in sterling—a move that proved prescient when London floated the pound later that month. "The first thing we want to avoid is catastrophe," Robbins says. But the possibility is always present. At any one time, Singer may have as much as $50 million directly invested in currencies as part of a total exposure to monetary vagaries that sometimes approaches $300 million.

Like all multinational companies, Singer lives in a rapidly changing world—and the changes aren't always benign. In . . . [1972], for instance, officials of the union that represents Singer workers in Monza, Italy, agreed with the Clydebank union that they would not permit Singer to switch production from one plant to the other in case of a strike. To keep track of such developments in an organized fashion, Edmund H. Damon, chief of the corporate-planning department, maintains elaborate charts coordinating each subsidiary's market potential (small, medium or large) and the degree of political-economic risk it faces (little, average or hazardous). . . . [In November 1971] after the government of South Africa moved to limit the imports of many companies there to only 20 percent of the 1969 level, Damon switched his South African assessment to small market potential, average risk, and sent out new instructions: to limit Singer's traditional presence, move the business toward indirect sales or a 50–50 cash-installment basis, and limit assets. And Singer South Africa (Pty.), Ltd., has done just that, eliminating all but five of its retail stores, shifting its business—and risk—to a dealer network and tightening credit policy.

Other, more basic changes are threatening the whole

Singer empire. In some of Singer's markets, the consumer sewing-machine business has reached a level of maturity that has begun to slow growth, and Singer executives grudgingly acknowledge that the future rests largely on their ability to export to the world the home sewing boom they helped create in the US. Meanwhile, the company is placing its foreign-investment eggs in what Kircher considers its major growth areas: home furniture, business machines and climate-control equipment. Shortly after the first of the year, the Business Machines Division will activate a small sales force in Europe to market its domestically successful computerized cash-register system. In the Far East Singer recently announced an agreement to form a joint venture with Hitachi, Ltd., the giant Japanese electronics firm, to market and eventually manufacture a wide range of business machines.

And there are still vast geographic markets virtually untapped—by Singer and other US multinationals as well. With trade restrictions relaxing, China and Eastern Europe loom as substantial long-term buyers of US-made goods. In September . . . [1972], Singer held its own one-company trade show in Warsaw. The exposition has thus far failed to ring Singer cash registers, but company officials are optimistic that the market eventually will open up. And in dealing with the Eastern bloc, Kircher clearly counts on the same principals that have sustained Singer through 118 years in foreign markets. "It may sound a bit platitudinous," he says, "but you must satisfy any government that the totality of your business is to be of benefit to the country. Sometimes, you must sacrifice short-term gains to convince them, but if you don't you're just not going to last."

A Dose of Their Own Medicine

Platitudinous or not, that statement could serve as the public credo of any multinational company—and it has convinced such veteran observers as Courtney Brown, former dean of the Columbia Business School, that global business is in fact good for the world. Indeed, he says, it is "the hoped-for force that will ultimately provide a means of unifying and reconciling the aspirations of mankind." Frank Church, for one, is skeptical of such grandiose claims, promising "a real investigative effort" to find out just what multinational companies really do in the world. But even as the battle lines are drawn, the tide of history continues to run with the global businessmen—and thus far the only workable response has been a dose of their own medicine. In Japan, for instance, domestic manufacturers have slashed Singer's share of the sewing-machine market from 50 percent forty years ago to 5 percent or less today. "We took a lesson," says Hiroshi Iyori, chief of the international section of Japan's Fair Trade Commission. "We too are building multinational enterprises."

MULTINATIONALS AND ACCOUNTABILITY [3]

Most managers of multinational enterprises approach the issue of social responsibility with a touch of genuine indignation.

They see themselves as engaged in an unending progress of adapting to the requirements of various jurisdictions, modifying their practices and curbing their preferences to conform to the demands of sovereign states.

From time to time, they may avoid the impact of some sovereign command by moving beyond the sovereign's reach or they may find themselves navigating between the conflicting and irreconcilable commands of different states.

But most managers will assert with conviction that illegal evasion is comparatively rare, especially when measured against the practices of indigenously-owned competitors. Insofar as there is evidence in this obscure and murky field, there is no reason to reject that generalization.

[3] Reprint of article by Raymond Vernon, professor, Harvard Business School. New York *Times*. p F 12. N. 18, '73. © 1973 by The New York Times Company. Reprinted by permission.

I see very little progress, however, in the formulation of an operational concept of social responsibility. The very discussion of social responsibility may well have sharpened the sensibilities of some of those who in any case were disposed to identify themselves with social needs; but I doubt that it has done much more.

The hard questions still remain unanswered. Should businessmen who produce a poison, such as cigarettes, liquidate a business that is both legal and profitable? Should businessmen whose facilities pollute the atmosphere take on the extra costs of prevention, even though the step may threaten their competitive position in the market?

The problem of the multinational enterprise in defining its social responsibilities is compounded even further. It is not inevitable that the social objectives of one country will be in conflict with the social objectives of another.

But conflict is not always avoidable in such matters as full employment, access to raw materials, balance-of-payment stability and national defense. In such cases, whose social objectives are to be served?

Apart from conflicts in the social objectives of nations, there may also be conflicts between what is good for mankind as a whole and what is good for each country taken one at a time.

I have no great expectations of improving the social performance of multinational enterprises by defining and inculcating concepts of social responsibility. But I see real possibilities in a narrower and more explicit approach, namely, increasing the social accountability of such enterprises.

The social accountability of the multinational enterprise would be achieved if appropriate social institutions were in a position to make judgments regarding the adequacy of the performance of the enterprises, and were in a position to take remedial measures when they saw some lack. To advance the idea of social accountability, however, one has to develop a set of institutions that for the most part do not exist today.

The range of problems involved is as broad as the field in industrial policy, a notoriously wider-ranging subject.

It includes such issues as tax policies for business, subsidization policies for industrial innovation or regional development, policies toward competition and monopoly, and policies in labor relations.

Beyond these well-trod areas of industrial policy, moreover, there are also questions that apply especially to the multinational enterprise.

These include defining the rights and obligations of multinational enterprise in invoking the powers or responding to the commands of sovereign states, when the interests of some other state are vitally involved.

In the field of taxation, several objectives would presumably be high on an international agenda, each of them requiring highly technical and detailed agreements. One would be to ensure that multinational enterprises did not slip between the taxing jurisdictions, that is, to ensure that their aggregate income was adequately taxed in some jurisdiction.

A second objective would be to avoid gross inequities in the distribution of taxable income among the various affiliates of any multinational enterprise, ensuring that a profit which ought to be attributed to one subsidiary is not assigned in effect to another.

And a third objective would be to protect the multinational enterprise itself from being caught between the scissors of the taxing jurisdictions.

The issue of national subsidies also promises to grow more acute.

The problems of international competition and monopoly power offer still another field for action. The emergence of the multinational enterprise has had some fundamental implications in this field.

In any case, it is no longer realistic to address the problems of oligopolistic practices on a country-by-country basis; in oil, chemicals, electronics, automobiles, copper, aluminum and other major industries, the oligopolistic structure is global.

Once again, some fairly specialized agreements and specialized apparatus are called for, covering such problems as the sorting out of jurisdictions, the collection of information, and the institution of effective remedies.

The labor relations field may demand a quite different approach. In this case, the growth of multinational enterprises has stimulated its own countervailing force, manifested by the strengthening of various international labor unions.

Labor groups are not the only national entities that have a need to know something about the operations of affiliates which lie outside their own national arena. Governmental agencies, public investor, consumer watchdog groups, and other national interests also have such needs from time to time.

As matters now stand, each national jurisdiction collects the data it needs, limiting itself as a rule to the activities of the affiliates in its jurisdiction.

One of the most difficult problems to be faced in increasing the social accountability of multinational enterprises is how to place a layer of insulation between parent enterprises and their national governments.

The delicacy of this problem is obvious. Governments are quite unlikely to accept self-denying ordinances of this sort unless the reciprocal advantages are crystal clear.

If international agreements could be reached in some of the fields mentioned—such as taxation, competition policy, and corporate disclosure—it might be possible for some of the participants to agree among themselves that in such areas the jurisdiction of each stopped at its national borders.

VI. THE COMING CORPORATE CONSCIENCE

EDITOR'S INTRODUCTION

Since Campaign GM (see Section III), there is no doubt that corporations are aware of a new pressure that must be faced in executive suites. Running corporations is no longer a "public be damned" operation. The revelations of the Nixon impeachment investigation have shown how politics can make some corporations irresponsible. Consumer advocates, environmental groups, and government agencies—city, state and Federal—along with other entities have made their influence felt. How are corporations responding to the pressure?

A *Business Week* article shows the role of institutional investors—commercial and nonprofit corporations that have substantial investments in other corporations—in insisting upon corporate responsibility through their control of blocks of shares. And in the final selection Charles N. Stabler provides specific examples of corporations concerned not only with their image but with the betterment of society.

INSTITUTIONAL INVESTORS AND CORPORATE RESPONSIBILITY [1]

Aetna Life & Casualty, a proper old insurance company with $1.5 billion in common stocks and no known radicals on its board, cast its proxies four times last year against the managements of companies in which it holds stock. Aetna supported stockholder resolutions that called for disclosing business activities in South Africa, ending investment in the

[1] Reprint of "Institutions That Balk at Antisocial Management." *Business Week*. p 66-7. Ja. 19, '74. Reprinted from the January 19, 1974 issue of *Business Week* by special permission. © 1974 by McGraw-Hill, Inc.

South African territory of Namibia, publicizing political contributions and lobbying, and hiring an outside auditor. It will vote against management again this year whenever companies in its portfolio fail to live up to their social responsibilities, Aetna spokesmen say calmly.

Aetna is not the only corporation or institution currently gearing up for the annual attempt to use proxy power at spring stockholder meetings. Other commercial institutional investors that have either voted proxies against management for social ends or have established high-level committees empowered to recommend such votes include Bank of America, First National City Bank, Morgan Guaranty Trust, Northwestern National Bank of Minneapolis, Prudential Insurance, Travelers Insurance, Equitable Life Assurance, Teachers Insurance & Annuity Association (TIAA), Massachusetts Financial Services, Scudder, Stevens & Clark, and Phillips-Van Heusen (whose committee on corporate accountability makes decisions for stocks held by the company's pension fund).

A small but growing group, these companies explain their new activism in terms made familiar by the churches and foundations that preceded them.

"Our primary investment purpose is financial return," says Robert B. Nicholas, Aetna's vice president for corporate planning. "But once you have bought a company's stock, you assume the responsibility of a shareholder." Adds William C. Greenough, chairman of nonprofit TIAA: "In its supporting and nudging role, the institutional investor has access to a potent lever to move the American corporation—the voting of corporate shares." Failure to use this lever leaves "a vacuum in the responsible exercise of corporate power," he says.

The Issues

This year the companies will have plenty to exercise their power about, warns Elliot J. Weiss, whose Investor Responsibility Research Center, Inc. (IRRC), a research group formed by universities and foundations to analyze corporate-responsibility issues, includes most of the activist institutions among its subscribers. Weiss expects the heaviest volume of social-responsibility proposals to date, especially stockholder demands that companies publicize the minority hiring and promotion data they give the Equal Employment Opportunities Commission [EEOC]. The Glide Foundation, which supports San Francisco's Glide Memorial Church, has already voted to file such resolutions with American Home Products, Celanese, Schering-Plough, Southern California Edison, Southern Company and Transamerica.

Other topics coming up at 1974 annual meetings, Weiss notes, are strip mining, political contributions, production of atrocious military weapons (with Honeywell, General Electric, and Rockwell International the prime targets), business activities in Latin America, Ireland, and the Middle East, environmental and energy policies, and disclosure of investments in South Africa and Rhodesia.

Most institutional investors, of course, will leave these hot issues strictly alone. They agree with former Securities and Exchange Commission Chairman William J. Casey, who maintains: "I doubt very much that money managers have the right to use funds committed to their trust to impose their social or political objectives on other shareholders."

The Investment Company Institute quotes Casey in its guidelines to members on how to deal with social responsibility criteria. It adds, however, that corporate-responsibility issues should be considered investment matters when they involve management's responsiveness to change.

Indeed, even those companies committed to proxy action move with conspicuous care, emphasizing that they plan no wholesale assault against management on all social-responsibility issues. Aetna, for instance, supported management last year against two other stockholder resolutions dealing with South African investments because it felt the two companies were handling the problems intelligently. And it abstained on a proposal demanding the appointment of outside directors after the company president assured Aetna Chairman John H. Filer that outsiders would be appointed voluntarily.

In this way, this assurance itself dramatizes the institutional investors' clout. It is rare for a stockholder proposal to pass, or even to get 10 percent of the vote, but most managements take notice when a substantial group of stockholders object to their policies—and doubly so when the objectors wield power in the financial community.

Scudder, Stevens & Clark, which supported a few social-issues resolutions for the first time last year, abstained on others they felt were badly drawn, even though they favored them. In such cases, the investment firm speaks informally to management, says John L. Casey, a senior vice president.

Most of the newly activist corporations agree with Casey that the 1973 proxy season was the "getting-to-know-you year, when we repeatedly found issues a lot more complicated than they first appeared." They agree also with Scudder senior vice president W. Russell Peabody that . . . [in 1974] they know more and expect to function more effectively.

"We've identified nine sensitive issues likely to come up in stockholder resolutions and have told our analysts to buck them automatically to our top committee," Casey says. The sensitive nine: disclosure, political and charitable contributions, fair employment and employee safety, restrictions on investment powers, environment, military contracts, director qualifications, shareholder voting procedures, and charter amendments.

Other subjects may emerge this month and next as stockholders file proposals under the SEC rule requiring filing at least seventy days before the issue date of the previous year's proxy.

The Motives

The decision to vote for or against these proposals will involve corporate self-interest as well as morality, the activist investors concede freely. Lawsuits and bad publicity damage profits, they note, and the management that ignores this effect raises questions about its competence.

"If a company has a 'public be damned' attitude in this day and age, one could infer that the management is not too sharp," says Philip R. Reynolds, senior vice president for finance at Travelers Insurance Company, whose portfolio holds more than $1 billion in common stocks. Other officials cite the EEOC settlement that cost American Telephone & Telegraph Company $38 million, the EEOC suits against General Motors, Ford, General Electric, and Sears, Roebuck, and the less publicized EEOC complaints against 160 other companies.

Says Robert Heisterberg, trust department vice president of the Bank of America, which manages stocks worth some $6 billion: "We have a high level of awareness about issues and how they will affect corporate performance. I tend to look at the implicit social contract of the corporate form of organization as a permanent part of the investment environment."

The Decisions

Whether undertaken for moral or financial reasons, weighing the social merits of a stockholder's proposal requires hard work. "Several hundred employee hours were spent reviewing the question, mailing documents to owners, tabulating results, and voting the proxies," says Peter A. Heegaard, vice president of Northwestern National Bank of Minneapolis, of its 1973 decision to oppose the appointment of a public director to the board of a public utility. "It would be only honest to say that the trust investment committee experienced new pressures and anxieties in dealing with the question." The bank polled the owners, Heegaard says, because "the presence of an interlocking director relationship made it especially important that the issue be debated fully."

Among corporate institutional investors, the pioneer activist was probably TIAA which began voting its proxies on a social-responsibility basis three years ago. Last year TIAA and its affiliated College Retirement Equities Fund backed shareholder proposals calling on Caterpillar Tractor, General Electric, and IBM to disclose their South African employment practices, on Eastman Kodak and ITT to disclose political contributions, and on Ford to disclose efforts to promote auto safety.

No other company has taken action on so many major fronts—in fact, no other company will even identify the managements it has opposed—but the trend is moving in TIAA's direction.

The Institute of Life Insurance, which omits proxy voting from the list of social-responsibility areas on which its members report, is considering including the subject on its next list, says Stanley Karson, director of ILI's Clearinghouse on Corporate Social Responsibility. The American Bankers Association has already come out for an activist position. "If controversial items are on the agenda and the trust institution has a majority or large minority interest, the shares should be voted in person," it instructs.

And here and there some institutional investors go so far as to quote Yale law professor John G. Simon, whose 1972 book, *The Ethical Investor*, laid down guidelines for Yale's own investment policies. "If the power of institutional investors is strong enough to control the outcome of corporate policy disputes," he wrote, "it underlines the extent to which investors, by failing to oppose socially injurious practices, may be said to cause them."

SOCIAL INVOLVEMENT: A GROWING CONCERN [2]

What is a corporation's job?

Five or ten years ago, any business executive worth his salt would have answered without hesitation: A corporation's job is to make money for its owners. In the process, it presumably creates employment and satisfies the needs of its customers. But the central goal is profit.

Today, though, that answer is rapidly becoming an anachronism. Corporations are still supposed to produce profit, but more and more executives share the sentiments expressed in a directive sent recently to local plant managers and supervisors of Owens-Illinois Inc.: "It is not enough merely to make a good product, deliver it at a good price and earn a good profit."

What is enough? For an increasing number of companies, the answer—in theory, at least—is to help clean the air and water, to provide jobs for minorities, to contribute money and talent to the solution of urban problems, to be more helpful to consumers and, in general, to help enhance the quality of life for everyone. At long last, it seems, the corporation is developing a social conscience.

Even now, the appropriateness of that development is a matter of debate. Economist Milton Friedman, for one, still argues that the corporation's responsibility is to produce profits and that the cost of corporate social goals amounts to a hidden tax on workers, customers and shareholders. [See "Social Responsibility and Corporate Policy Making in Section II.] . . . [In 1971] the board of governors of the Investment Company Institute, the trade association of the mutual fund industry, approved a set of guidelines to help fund managers find "enlightened" companies to invest in. But the board concluded that, in the end, "the primary responsibility of the investment company and its manage-

[2] Reprint of "For Many Corporations, Social Responsibility Is Now a Major Concern," by Charles N. Stabler, staff reporter. *Wall Street Journal.* p 1+. O. 26, '71. Reprinted with the permission of *The Wall Street Journal,* © Dow Jones & Company, Inc. 1971.

ment is to produce for its shareholders the optimum financial return" and that "this overriding principle should continue to be the fundamental basis for decisions on purchase, sale and holding of securities."

As for corporations themselves, there are still many that haven't succumbed to the notion that they're obliged to do anything but turn a profit. Others profess a social conscience but don't really mean it; they just recognize a public relations fad when they see it.

Behind the Ballyhoo

But behind the ballyhoo of antilittering campaigns, self-congratulatory advertisements and hot air from all sides, some major corporations are taking steps that they contend represent sincere efforts to gear social dimensions into their day-to-day operations. So far, the vast majority of these actions are in the realm of dealing with minorities. For example:

Chase Manhattan Bank now demands that its young executives make special efforts to counsel minority-owned businesses and community groups on financial matters.

General Electric plant managers are required to report regularly their percentage of nonwhite employees compared to the percentage of nonwhites in their areas. They also must submit five-year plans for increasing minority employment.

Atlantic Richfield has instructed its managers to hire nonwhite job applicants ahead of equally qualified whites. "I still get a report on my desk every quarter indicating the minority balance in all parts of the company," says Thornton F. Bradshaw, president. "When an area is lagging, I do something about it."

In Chicago, Standard Oil of Indiana recently announced it will insist on "an affirmative action program" to provide jobs for minority construction workers and contractors in building a $100 million, eighty-story building. The work force of the contractors must be 34 percent black, a rarity in the construction trades, and the company can cancel contracts if it isn't.

Intentions Aren't Enough

All this may sound simple enough to do. But for a big corporation, it can be a complex undertaking. Simply announcing an intention to "do good" isn't enough. Many companies, for instance, launched all sorts of "special projects" aimed at helping minorities after the urban riots of the mid-1960s. All too often, though, they were lacking in any long-term commitment. Most were ill-planned and quickly dropped.

"We are slowly moving to the real world from our earlier, overconfident rhetoric," says Thomas M. McMahon Jr., executive vice president of Chase Manhattan Bank. "All the way up and down the line, corporate responsibility must be treated as an integral corporate goal, just like profitability or efficiency."

In taking such a step, altruism is rarely the true motive. Most executives acknowledge they are acting from "enlightened self-interest." They see changing public opinion, growing pressure from activist groups and the threat of ever-tightening regulation of hiring, pollution and product safety as good reasons to take the initiative themselves. As economist Paul A. Samuelson has put it: "To advance the good cause, one must not expect too much of altruism."

The fact that corporate social involvement often begins as a public relations gesture doesn't particularly disturb the critics. "Corporations are still thinking pretty much in terms of their public image," says Frank White, director of the corporate information center of the National Council of Churches. But he adds: "That's not necessarily bad. If it starts out as public relations, at least it shows concern."

For many companies, the first step in formalizing a social

commitment is to put somebody in charge of "public affairs." The Public Affairs Council, a Washington-based group, estimates there are now more than two hundred corporate public affairs directors, compared with only a handful a few years ago.

Often the person holding such a title is merely a recycled public relations man with little contact with top officers of the company and little effect on policy. "The standard situation is that the public affairs director is not a guy who talks to the chairman or the president or even the executive vice president," says Michael Taylor, an official of the Council on Economic Priorities, a nonprofit group that reports on corporate practices in social areas.

Yet even Mr. Taylor doesn't fault the dedication of most public affairs directors. "These are motivated guys who do have some really strong commitments. If they can get in a position of influence they can motivate everybody else."

Some have professional backgrounds that equip them well for the role of counseling corporations. Wayne E. Thompson, senior vice president and public affairs chief of Dayton Hudson Corporation, a Minneapolis-based department store chain, is a former city manager. Samuel C. Convissor, director of urban affairs for RCA, worked in Federal antipoverty programs and for the city of Newark, New Jersey. Phillip T. Drotning, director of urban affairs for Standard Oil of Indiana, has written extensively on corporate responsibility.

Other companies are establishing high-level committees to keep tabs on social issues. General Motors, the target of proxy moves aimed at forcing it to become more socially involved, had appointed some of its directors to a public responsibility committee. It also has added a black activist to the board. CPC International Inc., a large food company (Skippy peanut butter, Mazola margarine, Karo syrup), recently named a group of outsiders headed by Bruce Palmer, president of the Better Business Bureaus, as a committee on corporate responsibility. It now is appraising the company's performance.

Such appraisals are of little value unless they lead to action. But advocates of change see genuine hope in the fact that some companies now are actually approaching social-interest areas with the tools of modern management, fitting their social goals into the corporate system of planning, reports and incentives. When General Electric set out to deal with racism within the company, for example, it started with what it called "a systems analysis of the total company action and response"—in other words, a look at not just what the company says it's doing but at what it's really doing.

Praise From a Critic

Now, less than three years later, the program is described as "the most comprehensive one of its kind that we know of in the corporate world" by Milton Moscowitz, editor of *Business and Society,* a newsletter that reports on corporate social involvement and is frequently critical of companies' shortcomings. (Oddly enough, though, GE refuses to disclose its actual percentage of nonwhite employment. A spokesman says, "The rate of overall minority additions to the work force accelerated; and, importantly, movement into professional and managerial ranks became quite noticeable.")

Despite some progress, though, corporations still have far to go to become deeply involved in social issues.

"In terms of levels of effort, looking at 1971 against, say, 1965, there has been movement. Consciousness has been raised and the subject (of social involvement) now is a respectable one," observes Mr. Taylor of the Council on Economic Priorities. "But in relation to what realistically and economically could be done, there are still some very severe gaps."

Corporate executives agree. "We can't paint too rosy a picture," says a spokesman for CPC International. "We are trying, but it's not easy when you have to move an organization of thirty thousand people."

Standard of Indiana's Mr. Drotning, looking back over the past five years, says: "My own feeling is that we've been dispensing Band-Aids. We've used corporate resources to deal with symptoms of urban problems without really getting to the basic causes."

Not Meeting the Problem

For example, Mr. Drotning says, Standard of Indiana shared in a Chicago program aimed at training 15,000 high school dropouts who were considered hard-core unemployed. But while training of those 15,000 was under way, 45,000 others dropped out of Chicago schools—making it apparent that the salvage effort wasn't really solving the problem. Now Standard Oil, along with CNA Financial and Sears, Roebuck, is assisting community efforts to improve the schools so dropouts will be less likely in the first place.

One important measure of the commitment of companies to social causes is the amount of money they are willing to donate, and at the moment that amount is less than impressive. Under Federal tax law, they are allowed to deduct from their taxable income donations of up to 5 percent of profits. But currently it's estimated that overall corporate philanthropy amounts to only about 1 percent of profits annually. If corporations all gave the maximum 5 percent, following the lead of Dayton-Hudson, Cummins Engine and a few other companies, they could "create four or five new Ford Foundations," one analyst figures.

Of course, many social projects undertaken by corporations have ended in disappointment, sometimes costly disappointment. One was the effort made by Boise Cascade Corporation to promote minority enterprise in the heavy-construction industry.

In 1967, Boise Cascade got together with a black-owned construction firm to form Boise-Burnett Corporation. Boise furnished financial backing, chiefly to provide the bonding capacity that is important to contractors, but had nothing to do with the management of the company. "They did not want us in it," says a Boise Cascade spokesman. "They wanted to do their own thing, and they did."

The idea was to enable Boise-Burnett to take on major development and construction projects. "The objective was half social and half profit—an investment with social implications."

At one time, Boise-Burnett had twenty projects going, the spokesman recalls. But then it began running into problems —cost overruns, delays, extra carrying costs and budgets going awry. The problem, says the spokesman, was that there "just aren't enough skilled minority people in the construction trades."

. . . [In 1971], although the operation was still functioning, Boise Cascade's accountants decided it was time to try to measure the corporation's potential losses. The result was a substantial writedown—a charge against income—in the second quarter. Other troubled Boise Cascade operations accounted for about half the company's total pretax writedown of $78 million, but a company official says Boise-Burnett accounted for the remainder. After taxes, the total writedown amounted to $44 million, equivalent to $1.44 a share.

Unhappy Shareholders

"Our shareholders were not too happy," concedes the spokesman. "After all, it's not our [management's] money."

Still, it's a rare chairman or president of a major company these days who hasn't, in speeches or in messages to stockholders, committed his company to social goals as well as economic ones.

"The philosophical underpinnings of corporations are changing," A. R. Marusi, president and chairman of Borden Inc., told a recent meeting of the National Association of Manufacturers' urban affairs committee, which he heads.

"The fulfillment of valid, rational human needs in a viable, economic way is becoming as much a concern as profit."

Phillip I. Blumberg, . . . [now dean of the University of Connecticut School of Law], specializes in corporate responsibility issues, characterizes some such talk as mere "felicitous rhetoric." But he adds:

The vital significance of such statements is that the objective of service to the society, which such business spokesmen are applying to business, inevitably will become the objective which the public generally will first accept as an appropriate role for business, subsequently come to expect and ultimately to demand.

[For a statement of Dean Blumberg's views, see "Corporate Responsibility and Environmental Abuse" in Section II.]

Who Must Pay?

A determination to play some sort of social role still leaves many questions unanswered. Who pays for social projects—the stockholders through lower dividends? Customers through higher prices? Workers through foregone wage increases? Probably everyone. Yet some corporate executives now are arguing that this search for an economic rationale for social involvement may be not so difficult as it appears.

For example, John R. Bunting, president of First Pennsylvania Corporation, a socially involved Philadelphia bank holding company, thinks the fear of shareholder complaints is largely a myth.

"Shareholders do not seem to react adversely to aggressive corporate social policies," he said recently in a speech. Moreover, he said, "social involvement has clear immediate advantages for a company that we do not often articulate."

For example, it may avert harassment by critics and thereby save management time. "I can think of few more foolish expenditures of salary dollars than having the corporate secretary and public relations officers, not to mention the chairman of the board, spending hours debating a second-year law student who owns three shares," he says.

Secondly, social involvement will help attract the "best young talent" to the corporate payroll, he says. "Finally, 'doing something' tends to energize the whole corporation and the revitalizing spirit generalizes easily to all corporate activities."

BIBLIOGRAPHY

An asterisk (*) preceding a reference indicates that the article or a part of it has been reprinted in this book.

BOOKS AND PAMPHLETS

Anshen, Melvin, ed. Managing the socially responsible corporation. Macmillan. '74.

Bank of America. Bibliography: corporate responsibility for social problems, vol. 3. The Bank. P. O. Box 37000. San Francisco, Calif. 94137. '74.

Barnet, R. J. and Müller, R. E. Global reach: the power of the multinational corporations. Simon & Schuster. '74.
    Shorter version: New Yorker. 50:53-6+, 100+. D. 2-9, '74.

Baumol, W. J. and others. A new rationale for corporate social policy. Heath. '70.

Bell, Daniel. The coming of post-industrial society: a venture in social forecasting. Basic Books. '73.

Berle, A. A. and Means, G. C. The modern corporation and private property. rev. ed. Harcourt. '68.

*Blumberg, P. I. Corporate responsibility and environmental abuse; introductory statement at Round Table of the Association of American Law Schools, Chicago, December 28, 1970.
    Mimeographed. Copies not available for distribution.

Blumberg, P. I. Corporate responsibility in a changing society. Boston University. School of Law. 765 Commonwealth Ave. Boston, Mass. 02215. '72.

Bosen, H. R. Social responsibilities of the businessman. Harper. '53.

Brooks, J. N. The go-go years. Weybright and Talley. '73.

Bunting, J. R. From Adam Smith to Phase III. First Pennsylvania Corporation. 15th and Chestnut Sts. Philadelphia, Pa. 19102. '73.

Capitman, W. G. Panic in the boardroom: new social realities shake old corporate structures. Doubleday. '73.

Chamberlain, N. W. The limits of corporate responsibility. Basic Books. '73.

Chandler, A. D. Jr. and Salisbury, Stephen. Pierre S. Du Pont and the making of the modern corporation. Harper. '71.

Childs, M. W. and Cater, Douglass. Ethics in a business society. Harper. '54.

*Cohen, M. F. The corporation within the community; address before the Economic Club of Detroit on January 27, 1969. Mimeographed. Copies not available for distribution.

Cohen, Peter. The gospel according to the Harvard Business School. Doubleday. '73.

Cohn, Jules. The conscience of the corporations: business and urban affairs. Johns Hopkins Press. '71.

Committee for Economic Development. Research and Policy Committee. Social responsibilities of business corporations; a statement on national policy, June 1971. The Committee for Economic Development. 477 Madison Ave. New York 10022. '71.

Cook, F. J. The corrupted land: the social morality of modern America. Macmillan. '66.

Corson, J. J. Business in the humane society. McGraw-Hill. '71.

Council on Economic Priorities. Guide to corporations, a social perspective; researched and written by Joe Zalkind and others; ed. by Stephen Moody and Lee Stephenson. Swallow Press. '74.

Council on Religion and International Affairs. Consultation on Corporate Responsibility, Airlie House, 1972. The multinational corporation and social policy [with] special reference to General Motors in South Africa; ed. by R. A. Jackson. Praeger. '74.

Cox, E. F. and others. The Nader report on the Federal Trade Commission. Richard W. Baron Publishing Company. '69.

Crusz, Rienzi, comp. Ralph Nader: a bibliography, April 15, 1973. University of Waterloo. Dana Porter Arts Library. Reference Department. Waterloo, Ontario, Canada N2L 3G1. '73.

Davis, Keith and Blomstrom, R. L. Business, society and environment: social power and social response. 2d ed. McGraw-Hill. '71.

Demaris, Ovid. Dirty business: the corporate political money-power game. Harpers Magazine Press. '74.

Dierkes, Meinolf and Bauer, R. A. eds. Corporate social accounting. Praeger. '73.

Drucker, P. F. Management: tasks, responsibilities, practices. Harper. '74.

Eels, R. S. F. The government of corporations. Free Press. '62.

Evan, W. M. Organizational experiments. Harper. '71.

First Pennsylvania Corporation. Annual report. The Corporation. 15th and Chestnut Sts. Philadelphia, Pa. 19101. '72.

Freemont-Smith, M. R. Philanthropy and the business corporation. Russell Sage. '72.

Friedman, Milton. Capitalism and freedom. University of Chicago Press. '62.

Galbraith, J. K. Economics and the public purpose. Houghton. '73.

Galbraith, J. K. The new industrial state. 2d rev. ed. Houghton. '71.

Gilbert, Michael, ed. The modern business enterprise: selected readings. Penguin. '72.

Gilliland, C. E. Jr. ed. Readings in business responsibility. D. H. Mark. '69.

Ginzberg, Eli and Yoholem, A. M. eds. Corporate lib: women's challenge to management. Johns Hopkins University Press. '73.

Goldston, Eli and others. The American business corporation; new perspectives on profit and purpose. M.I.T. Press. '72.

Goodman, Walter. All honorable men: corruption and compromise in American life. Little. '63.

*Goodwin, R. N. The American condition. Doubleday. '74.
    Originally appeared in part in New Yorker. 49:35-40+. Ja. 21; 36-44+. Ja. 28; 48+. F. 4, '74.

Green, M. J. ed. The monopoly makers: Ralph Nader's study group report on regulation and competition. Grossman. '73.

Haas, J. J. Corporate social responsibilities in a changing society. Theo Gaus' Sons. '73.

Hacker, Andrew, ed. The corporation take-over. Harper. '64.

Heald, Morrell. The social responsibilities of business, company, and community, 1900-1960. Press of Case Western Reserve University. '70.

Heilbroner, R. L. and others. In the name of profit. Doubleday. '72.

Hodges, L. H. The business conscience. Prentice-Hall. '63.

Humble, J. W. Social responsibility audit; a management tool for survival. Amacom. P. O. Box 509. Saranac Lake, N. Y. 12983. '73.

Jacoby, N. H. Corporate power and social responsibility: a blueprint for the future. Macmillan. '73.

Kahn, Herman, ed. The future of the corporation. Mason and Lipscomb. '74.

Larson, J. A. ed. The responsible businessman, business and society: readings from Fortune. Holt. '66.

Leinsdorf, David and Etra, Donald. Citibank: Ralph Nader's study group report on First National City Bank. Grossman. '74.

Linowes, D. F. The corporate conscience. Hawthorn. '74.

Liston, R. A. Who really runs America? Doubleday. '74.

Longstreth, Bevis and Rosenbloom, H. D. Corporate social responsibility and the institutional investor: a report to the Ford Foundation. Praeger. '73.

Manne, H. G. and Wallich, H. C. The modern corporation and social responsibility. American Enterprise Institute for Public Policy Research. 1150 17th St. N.W. Washington, D.C. 20036. '73.

Marquis, H. H. The changing corporate image. American Management Association. 135 W. 50th St. New York 10020. '70.

Mason, E. S. ed. The corporation in modern society. Atheneum. '66.

Mills, C. W. The power elite. Oxford University Press. '56.

Mintz, Morton and Cohen, J. S. America, Inc.: who owns and operates the United States? Dial. '71.

Moore, W. E. The conduct of the corporation. Random House. '62.

Moss, F. E. Initiatives in corporate responsibility. 92d Congress, 2d session. U.S. Gov. Ptg. Office. Washington, D.C. 20401. '72.

Mueller, R. K. Board life: realities of being a corporate director. Amacom. P. O. Box 509. Saranac Lake, N. Y. 12983. '74.

*Nader, Ralph. Campaign GM: a statement announcing Campaign GM to the press in Washington, D.C. on February 7, 1970. Center for Study of Responsive Law. P. O. Box 19367. Washington, D.C. 20036. '70. 8p. mimeo.

Nader, Ralph, ed. The consumer and corporate accountability. Harcourt. '73.

Nader, Ralph and Green, M. J. eds. Corporate power in America; Ralph Nader's Conference on Corporate Accountability, Washington, D.C., 1971. Grossman. '73.

Nader, Ralph and others, eds. Whistle blowing; report [of the] Conference on professional responsibility, Washington, D.C., 1971. Grossman. '72.

*New York Stock Exchange. You and the investment world. 2d ed. The Exchange. 11 Wall St. New York 10005. '72.

Nicholson, E. A. and others. Business responsibility and social issues. Merrill. '74.

Orren, Karen. Corporate power and social change: the politics of the life insurance industry. Johns Hopkins University Press. '74.

Peters, Charles and Taylor, Branch, eds. Blowing the whistle: dissent in the public interest. Praeger. '72.

Phelan, James and Pozen, Robert. The company state: Ralph Nader's study group report on Du Pont in Delaware. Grossman. '73.

Powers C. W. Social responsibility and investments. Abingdon. '71.

Reich, C. A. The greening of America: how the youth revolution is trying to make America livable. Random House. '70.

Ridgeway, James. The closed corporation: American universities in crisis. Random House. '68.

*Roche, J. M. The threat to American business; address before the Executive Club of Chicago, March 25, 1971. General Motors Corporation. 767 Fifth Ave. New York 10022. '71. 12p. mimeo.

Ross, J. E. and Kami, M. J. Corporate management in crisis: why the mighty fall. Prentice-Hall. '73.

Scheer, Robert. America after Nixon: the age of the multinationals. McGraw. '74.

Seidenberg, Robert. Corporate wives—corporate casualties? Amacom. P. O. Box 509. Saranac Lake, New York 12983. '73.

Sethi, S. P. ed. The unstable ground: corporate social policy in a dynamic society. Melville. '74.

Sethi, S. P. Up against the corporate wall; modern corporations and social issues of the seventies. 2d ed. Prentice-Hall. '74.

Simon, J. G. and others. The ethical investor: universities and corporate responsibility. Yale University Press. '72.

Sperber, N. H. and Lerbinger, Otto. Key to the executive head. Addison-Wesley. '75.

Tipper, Harry, Jr. The system and what you can do with it. Gambit. '73.

Townsend, Robert. Up the organization. Knopf. '70.

United Nations. Department of Economic and Social Affairs. Multinational corporations in world development. United Nations. Publishing Service. New York 10017. '73.

United States. Congress. Senate. Committee on Finance. Subcommittee on International Trade. Multinational corporation and the world economy; Feb. 26, 1973. 93rd Congress; 1st session. Supt. of Docs. Washington, D.C. 20402. '73.

United States. Congress. Senate. Committee on Finance. Subcommittee on International Trade. Multinational corporations, compendium of papers, Feb. 21, 1973. 93rd Congress, 1st session. The committee. '73.

United States. Congress. Senate. Select Committee on Small Business. Role of giant corporations; hearings before Subcommittee on Monopoly, on role of giant corporations in American and world economies. 92nd Congress, 1st session. Supt. of Docs. Washington D.C. 20402. '72.

Votaw, Dow and Sethi, S. P. The corporate dilemma; traditional values versus contemporary problems. Prentice-Hall. '73.

Walton, C. C. Corporate social responsibilities. rev. ed. Wadsworth. '68.

Wasserstein, Bruce and Green, M. J. With justice for some. Beacon. '70.
   Taming GM . . . Ford, Union Carbide, U.S. Steel, Dow Chemical. D. P. Riley. p 207-43.

Weissman, J. I. The social responsibilities of corporate management. (Yearbook of Business. Ser. 3, v 2) Hofstra University. School of Business. Hempstead, N. Y. 11550. '66.

Wellington Management Company. Corporate responsibility: the mutual fund shareholder speaks. The Company. P. O. Box 823. Valley Forge, Pa. 19482. '71.

Winslow, J. F. Conglomerates unlimited: the failure of regulation. Indiana University Press. '73.

PERIODICALS

American University Law Review. 23:263-311. Winter '73. Corporations and society: the remedy of federal and international incorporation. S. J. Rubin.

American University Law Review. 23:313-35. Winter '73. Multilaw. W. S. Barnes.

Annals of American Academy of Political and Social Science. 343:1-141. S. '62. The ethics of business enterprise. A. S. Miller, ed.

Annals of the American Academy of Political and Social Science. 403:1-152. S. '72. The multinational corporation; symposium. D. H. Blake, ed.

*Barron's. p 1+. My. 18, '70. Good for General Motors? Corporate enterprise is responsible solely to its owners. H. G. Manne.

Barron's. p 5+. O. 12, '70. Corporate militants: their lawsuit makes a case for sounder securities regulation. H. G. Manne.

Barron's. p 1. My. 17, '73. Who's responsible? What the anticorporate zealots are pushing is coercion. H. G. Manne.

Black Enterprise. 4:17-28. S. '73. Black directors on white boards. Lester Carson.

Boston University Law Review. 50:157-208. '70. Corporate responsibility and the social crisis. P. I. Blumberg.

Business and Society Review. 1:5-16. Spring '72. Milton Friedman responds [interview].

Business and Society Review. 1:54-6. Spring '72. The emerging public corporation. J. K. Galbraith.

Business and Society Review. 1:63-8. Spring '72. Reforming the corporation from within. D. E. Schwartz.

Business and Society Review. 5:35-9. Spring '73. Arthur Goldberg on public directors: an interview.

Business and Society Review. 8:59-64. Winter '73-'74. Federal chartering of corporations: an idea well worth forgetting. P. H. Aranson.

Business Horizons. 16:45-51. F. '73. The corporate responsibility officer: a new position on the organization chart. Henry Eilbirt and I. R. Parket.

Business Lawyer. 24:149-57. N. '68. Corporate decision-making and social control. A. A. Berle, Jr.

Business Lawyer. 24:165-71. N. '68. The future direction of the modern corporation. W. P. Gullander.

Business Lawyer. 26:513-26. N. '70. Corporate responsibility in the age of Aquarius. D. E. Schwartz.

Business Lawyer. 26:533-9. N. '70. The myth of corporate responsibility; or, Will the real Ralph Nader please stand up? H. G. Manne.

Business Lawyer. 27:1275-99. Jl. '72. Selected materials on corporate social responsibility. P. I. Blumberg.

Business Lawyer. 28:177-213. Mr. '73. Corporate social responsibility panel: the constituencies of the corporation and the role of the institutional investor. P. I. Blumberg and others.

Business Week. p 63-74. N. 1, '69. The war that business must win.

Business Week. p 82+. Ap. 11, '70. Pollution and the profit motive.

Business Week. p 86-7. F. 13, '71. Social activists switch to proxy power.

Business Week. p 52-5. F. 20, '71. Companies face an identity crisis.

Business Week. p 76+. My. 1, '71. The moral power of shareholders.

Business Week. p 58-9. Jl. 24, '71. Meet Ralph Nader's most outspoken critic [Henry G. Manne].

Business Week. p 32-5. Ja. 1, '72. Dow cleans up pollution at no net cost.

Business Week. p 79-80. Ja. 22, '72. The black message: business must do more.

Business Week. p 88-92. S. 23, '72. First attempts at a corporate "social audit."

Business Week. p 45. Ap. 28, '73. Consumers battle for board seats.

Business Week. p 25-6. Ag. 18, '73. The U.N. sizes up the global giants.

*Business Week. p 66-7. Ja. 19, '74. Institutions that balk at antisocial management.

Case Western Reserve Law Review. 20:825-73. '69. Tax and other legal aspects of business involvement in ghetto development programs.

Center Magazine. 5:26-79. Ja.-F. '72. The corporation and the quality of life.
    Conference: Robert Townsend, T. J. Jacobs, R. A. Bauer, J. J. Corson, R. S. F. Eells, C. R. Kemp, L. J. Carter, N. H. Jacoby, R. Parker.

Christian Century. 88:249-52. F. 24, '71. The Polaroid approach to South Africa. G. M. Houser.

*Christian Science Monitor. p 22. N. 19, '73. Help for workers who blow the whistle on employers. Lucia Mouat.

Christian Science Monitor. p 5. Ja. 8, '74. To the United States Congress: Institutional control of corporations could just prove to be a good thing. Richard Nenneman.

Christian Science Monitor. p 6. Ja. 15, '74. Who says U.S. industry is unresponsive to public? Richard Nenneman.

Christian Science Monitor. p 4. Ja. 21, '74. Multinational firms may face trouble. F. H. Guidry.

Christian Science Monitor. p 5. Mr. 7, '74. Latest in corporate learning centers: It's what we do here that counts. F. H. Guidry.

Christian Science Monitor. p 3. Je. 6, '74. Corporate conscience: shareholders gain. Kenneth McCormick.

Christian Science Monitor. p 5. Jl. 3, '74. Are the multinationals too big? G. E. Tweson.

Columbia Journal of Law and Social Problems. 10:15-46. Fall '73. The greening of the board room: reflections on corporate responsibility.
    Panel: J. Goldschmid, W. L. Cary, N. W. Chamberlain, R. O. Lehrman.

Columbia Journal of World Business. 6:59-64. Ja.-F. '71. The multinational corporation: measuring the consequences. R. B. Stobaugh.

Columbia Journal of World Business. 7:6-12. S.-O '72. National support of multinational ventures. W. G. Carter.

Conference Board Record. 4:9-12. N. '67. Business defines its social responsibilities. G. J. Finley.

Conference Board Record. 7:33-6. D. '70. The corporation and the public good. C. F. Stover.

Conference Board Record. 8:42-7. Ap. '71. Corporate responsibility and the environment. P. I. Blumberg.

Conference Board Record. 8:48-51. Ap. '71. Shareholder proposals as a vehicle of protest. H. C. Egerton.

Conference Board Record. 8:21-4. Jl. '71. The greening of American business. T. V. Learson.

Conference Board Record. 8:25-32. Jl. '71. Business leadership in social change. Holly MacNamee.

Conference Board Record. 8:38-40. Jl. '71. Realities v. rhetoric: the dilemma of social cost. R. L. Ash.

Conference Board Record. 8:48-52. Jl. '71. Can workers participate in management—successfully? Burton Teague.

Conference Board Record. 8:28-31. Ag. '71. Corporate accountability. A challenge to business. M. S. Armstrong.

Conference Board Record. 8:53-7. N. '71. New dimensions for boards of directors. S. C. Vance.

Conference Board Record. 9:42-3. F. '72. The more representative board. S. R. Pokempner.

Conference Board Record. 9:44-7. F. '72. Directors under pressure. Jeremy Bacon.

Congressional Record. (daily ed.) 120:S989-91. Ja. 18, '73. The multinational corporation: a perception of America. Frank Church.

Congressional Record. (daily ed.) 120:E1877-8. Mr. 27, '73. Eli Lilly & Co. of Indianapolis: meeting responsibilities to society.

Congressional Record. (daily ed.) 120:E4222-3. Je. 19, '73. Multinational corporations, their effect on the U.S. taxpayer. J. R. Tarick.

Congressional Record. (daily ed.) 120:S13660-1. Jl. 17, '73. Corporate responsibility and the consumers. Peter Jones.

Congressional Record. (daily ed.) 120:S17994-6. S. 28, '73. Political and economic implications of multinational corporations. I. S. Shapiro.

*Congressional Record. (daily ed.) 120:E6492-3. O. 15, '73. Black directorships. W. E. Fauntroy.

Congressional Record. (daily ed.) 120:S19713-15. O. 30, '73. The world corporation: new weight in an old balance. W. B. Wriston.

Cornell Law Review. 56:1-56. '70. The government of business corporations: critical reflections on the rule of "one share, one vote." D. L. Ratner.

Daedalus. 98:78-112. Winter '69. New prospects for American business. Eli Goldston.

*Financial Executive. 42:30-5. Mr. '74. Corporate support of private universities. David Packard.

Financial Executive. 42:36-44. Mr. '74. Private institutions in the public service. McGeorge Bundy.

Fortune. 78:88-91+. Ag. '68. Business wrestles with its social conscience. R. C. Albrook.

Fortune. 79:102-4+. Ap. '69. Business picks up the urban challenge. A. T. Demaree.

Fortune. 80:93-5+. S. '69. What business thinks. A. M. Louis.

Fortune. 81:114-17+. F. '70. Industry starts the big cleanup. John Davenport.

Fortune. 82:106-7+. O. '70. Why an outmoded ideology thwarts the new business conscience. G. C. Lodge.

Fortune. 82:104-6+. D. '70. How social responsibility fits the game of business. John McDonald.

Fortune. 83:144-7+. My. '71. The passion that rules Ralph Nader. Richard Armstrong.

Fortune. 85:99-101. Ja. '72. G.M.: the price of being "responsible." Peter Vanderwicken.

Fortune. 86:48-53+. Jl. '72. The proper role of United States corporations in South Africa. John Blashill.

*Fortune. 87:675-9+. Ap. '73. The "legal explosion" has left business shell-shocked. Eleanore Carruth.

Fortune. 87:114-17+. Je. '73. The hazards of "corporate responsibility." Gilbert Burck.

Fortune. 88:52-6+. Ag. '73. Multinational corporations in a tough new world. Sanford Rose.

Fortune. 88:59-62+. Ag. '73. How the multinationals play the money game. R. B. Stobaugh and S. M. Robbins.

Fortune. 88:74-9+. Ag. '73. Continental Can's intercontinental tribulations. Peter Vanderwicken.

*Fortune. 88:56. N. '73. The "responsible" corporation: benefactor or monopolist? [debate] Eli Goldston and Milton Friedman.

*Fortune. 88:179-80. D. '73. What goes on at the Harvard Business School. Andrew Tobias.
    Review of The gospel according to the Harvard Business School, by Peter Cohen.

George Washington Law Journal. 40:1-75. '71. Shareholder cause proposals: a technique to catch the conscience of the corporations. Stephen Schulman.

Georgetown Law Journal. 60:57-109. '71. Towards new corporate goals: co-existence with society. D. E. Schwartz.

Georgetown Law Journal. 61:71-149. '72. Federal chartering of corporations: an introduction. D. E. Schwartz.

Harper's Magazine. 243:61-7. Ag. '71. Stocks without sin. Walter Goodman.

Harvard Business Review. 36:77-86. Mr.-Ap. '58. Social audit of the enterprise. F. H. Blum.

Harvard Business Review. 36:41-50. S.-O. '58. The dangers of social responsibility. Theodore Levitt.

Harvard Business Review. 39:6-8+. Jl. '61. How ethical are businessmen? R. C. Baumhart.

Harvard Business Review. 39:53-61. S.-O. '61. Code of conduct for executives. R. W. Austin.

Harvard Business Review. 43:45-52. Jl.-Ag. '65. Who takes the responsibility for social change? R. W. Austin.

Harvard Business Review. 46:77-85. Jl. '68. Should business tackle society's problems. Hazel Henderson.

Harvard Business Review. 47:122-8. Ja. '69. The limits of black capitalism. F. D. Sturdivant.

Harvard Business Review. 47:4-6+. Mr. '69. Business has a war to win; excerpts from address, December 5, 1968. J. I. Miller.

Harvard Business Review. 47:49-60. Mr. '69. Toward professionalism in business management. K. R. Andrews.

Harvard Business Review. 47:83-92. My. '69. Making capitalism work in the ghettos. L. L. Allen.

Harvard Business Review. 47:84-9. S. '69. BURP and make money. Eli Goldston.

Harvard Business Review. 48:49-61. Ja. '70. Is the corporation next to fall? A. G. Athos.

Harvard Business Review. 48:68-82. Mr. '70. Is business meeting the challenge of urban affairs? Jules Cohn.

Harvard Business Review. 48:58-64. Jl. '70. Can an executive afford a conscience? A. Z. Carr.

Harvard Business Review. 48:43-55. S. '70. Top priority: renovating our ideology. G. C. Lodge.

Harvard Business Review. 48:131-42. N. '70. An anatomy of activism for executives. S. A. Culbert and J. M. Elden.

Harvard Business Review. 49:131-8. Ja. '71. Turn public problems to private account. R. C. Rockefeller.

Harvard Business Review. 49:4-6+. Mr. '71. Executives as community volunteers. D. H. Fenn, Jr.

Harvard Business Review. 49:37-47. Mr. '71. Moral issues in investment policy. B. G. Malkiel and R. E. Quandt.

Harvard Business Review. 49:82-90. My. '71. Toward managing social conflict. Hazel Henderson.

Harvard Business Review. 49:12-14+. S. '71. Who wants corporate democracy? D. W. Ewing.

Harvard Business Review. 49:22-4+. N. '71. Who wants employee rights? D. W. Ewing.

Harvard Business Review. 49:121-6. N. '71. Is business the source of new social values? O. A. Bremer.

Harvard Business Review. 51:37-48. Ja. '73. What is a corporate social audit? R. A. Bauer and D. H. Fenn, Jr.

Harvard International Law Journal. 15:71-125. '74. Multinational enterprise and racial non-discrimination: United States enforcement of an international human right. W. J. Dehner.

Institutional Investor. 4:25-33+. Jl. '70. Do institutional investors have a social responsibility? Peter Landau.

Journal of Accountancy. 136:62-70. S. '73. Measuring social responsibility: an empirical test. S. C. Dilley and J. J. Weygandt.

Journal of Law and Economics. 3:75-85. '60. Responsibility and the modern corporation. Wilber Katz.

Journal of Law and Economics. 13:185-221. '70. Separation of ownership and control in the modern corporation. Brian Hindley.

Journal of Law Reform. 5:68-86. '71. The shareholder's role in corporate social responsibility.

Journal of World Trade Law. 7:267-92. '73. The multinational corporation and the nation-state. A. S. Miller.

Law Center Bulletin (New York University School of Law). v 20, no 1:6-9. '73. A panel discussion on corporate responsibility.

Michigan Law Review. 69:419-538. '71. The public-interest proxy contest: reflections on Campaign GM. D. E. Schwartz.

Nation. 211:617-21. D. 14, '70. Politics by other means. Hazel Henderson.

Nation. 214:265-9. F. 28, '72. Corporate secrecy. Thomas De Baggio.

Nation. 216:173-6. F. 5, '73. The case for federal charters. Ralph Nader and M. J. Green.

National Review. 21:742-4. Jl. 29, '69. Business and black capitalism. John Chamberlain.

New Republic. 162:13-14. Ap. 25, '70. Whose business is business? R. W. Dietsch.

New Republic. 162:8-9. Je. 6, '70. Commotion at GM. L. J. Carter.

New Republic. 162:14-16. N. 14, '70. Business in government. M. J. Green.

*New Republic. 169:24-6. O. 13, '73. The managerial elite. M. J. Ulmer.
     Review of Economics and the public purpose, by J. K. Galbraith.

New Republic. 171:17-19. Jl. 6-13, '74. Beyond antitrust. Peter Barnes and Derek Shearer.

New Republic. 171:13-17. N. 2, '74. Perfecting the corporation: what comes after General Motors. J. K. Galbraith.

*New York Law Journal. p 1+. Ag. 9, '73. Reform of English company law. Martin Lipton.

New York. 3:35-8. D. 21, '70. The greening of James Roche. Chris Welles.

New York Review of Books. 15:4-6. Jl. 2, '70. Corporate responsibility for war crimes. George Wald.

New York Review of Books. 15:20-4. N. 19, '70. Power to the workers? Robert Dahl.

New York Review of Books. 16:20-5. F. 11, '71. The multinational corporation and the nation-state. R. L. Heilbroner.

New York Review of Books. 20:37-42. N. 29, '73. Owing your soul to the company store. Ralph Nader and Mark Green.

New York Times. p 59. Mr. 23, '70. Students vs. executives: a brisk dialogue. W. D. Smith.

New York Times. p 43. Ja. 15, '71. A code for professional integrity. Ralph Nader.

New York Times. p F 1. Ja. 24, '71. Needler: teaching the banks virtue. R. D. Hershey, Jr.

New York Times. p F 1. Ja. 24, '71. Reformer: urging business change [Ralph Nader]. Eileen Shanahan.

New York Times. p 14. Mr. 14, '71. Accounting for social progress. D. F. Linowes.

New York Times. p 45. Mr. 17, '71. Citizens of the corporation. Robert Dahl.

New York Times. p 1+. Ap. 4, '71. Investment return v. social role and concern. Marylin Bender.

New York Times. p F 1+. Ap. 4, '71. Universities' corporate voice. Marylin Bender.

New York Times. p F 7. Ap. 11, '71. Good guys and bad guys: institutions asked to consider morality. Eileen Shanahan.

New York Times. p 12. Ap. 18, '71. U.S. business should leave South Africa.

New York Times. p 56. My. 12, '71. Market place: weighing cost of Nader plan. Robert Metz.

New York Times. p 33. Ag. 4, '71. The greening of the board room. W. L. Cary.

New York Times. p E 3. N. 14, '71. A new breed of "criminal." Robert Reinhold.

New York Times. p 47. D. 2, '71. Regulating utilities—and us. Nicholas Johnson.

New York Times. p F 4. F. 20, '72. Corporate tokenism for women? Marylin Bender.

*New York Times. p F 1+. O. 29, '72. The role of outside directors. A. J. Goldberg.

New York Times. p F 1. Ja. 7, '73. Capitalism lives—even in Naderland. Marylin Bender.

New York Times. p F 17. Mr. 11, '73. Government is the real monopoly. Lee Loevinger.

New York Times. p 25. Mr. 11, '73. Religious groups use proxy power. E. B. Fiske.

New York Times. p F 14. Mr. 18, '73. New environmental executives.

New York Times. p F 14. Mr. 18, '73. Social measurement. A. B. Toan, Jr.

*New York Times. p 55-6. Ap. 2, '73. Corporate-responsibility groups broaden tactics. Marylin Bender.

New York Times. p 17. Jl. 30, '73. 4 to 6 giant companies being picked as federal target on discrimination. Eileen Shanahan.

New York Times. p F 1. Ag. 16, '73. The corporate political squeeze. M. C. Jensen.

New York Times. p F 11. Ag. 26, '73. Regulating the multinationals: fair play or anarchy? R. E. Mooney.

*New York Times. p F 12. Ag. 26, '73. An ombudsman for executives? W. M. Evan.

New York Times. p 65. S. 12, '73. Multinational companies defend role before U.N. Kathleen Teltsch.

New York Times. p 55. S. 18, '73. Multinational companies called agents of change. R. A. Wright.

New York Times. p 7. N. 11, '73. The management doctors. Ernest Holsendolph.

*New York Times. p F 12. N. 18, '73. Multinationals and accountability. Raymond Vernon.

New York Times. p 45. Ja. 8, '74. Business is "own worst enemy" to public, May's chairman says. Isadore Barmash.

New York Times. p 45. Ja. 26, '74. Church groups hit corporations. Eleanor Blau.

New York Times. p E 3. Ja. 27, '74. A look at the multinationals. Edward Cowan.

New York Times. p 29. Mr. 4, '74. The profit system and America's growth. R. C. Gerstenberg.

New York Times. p 49. Ap. 1, '74. Corporate support rises for minorities' education. Reginald Stuart.

New York Times. p 33. Ap. 5, '74. Mutinational morals. Leonard Silk.

*New York Times. p 43. Ap. 12, '74. Jobholders get chance to air gripes at Pitney-Bowes. Reginald Stuart.

New York Times. p 43. Ap. 17, '74. Against "Naderism." Anthony Harrigan.

New York Times. p 51. My. 4, '74. Annual reports: some progress on disclosure. J. H. Allan.

New York Times. p 3. My. 26, '74. The new snares facing outside directors. Lawrence Stessin.

*New York Times. p 39. Je. 18, '74. The work and the worker. Tom Wicker.

New York Times. p E 4. Je. 30, '74. Big business as everyman's villain. M. J. Green.

New York Times. p 1+. N. 11, '74. Work democracy tested at Scandinavian plants. Agis Salpukas.

New York Times Magazine. p 32-3+. S. 13, '70. The social responsibility of business is to increase its profits. Milton Friedman.

New York Times Magazine. p 20-2+. Mr. 18, '73. The multinationals: giants beyond flag and country. H. D. Shapiro.

*New Yorker. 46:40-2+. Je. 20, '70. Our footloose correspondents. E. J. Kahn Jr.

New Yorker. 47:138+. O. 9, '71. The marts of trade. John Brooks.

Newsweek. 75:75-6. Ap. 27, '70. The annual meeting under fire.

Newsweek. 75:109. Ap. 27, '70. Taking stock: Campaign GM.

Newsweek. 76:58-60. Ag. 31, '70. The board under fire.

Newsweek. 77:88. Mr. 29, '71. Corporate giants. P. A. Samuelson.

Newsweek. 77:74-8+. My. 24, '71. American corporations under fire.

*Newsweek. 80:96-8+. N. 20, '72. Global companies: too big to handle?

Public Interest. p 72-84. Spring '69. The idea of a social report. Daniel Bell.

Public Interest. p 5-32. Summer '71. The corporation and society in the 1970's. Daniel Bell.

Public Policy. 21:303-17. Summer '73. Social responsibility and economic efficiency. K. J. Arrow.

Ramparts. 12:21-3+. Mr. '74. How far can a lone ranger [Ralph Nader] ride? William Greider.

St. John's Law Review. 45:764-71. '71. Proxy power and social goals: how Campaign GM succeeded. D. E. Schwartz.

Saturday Review. 53:55. Ag. 8, '70. Profit alone is not enough: interview with James M. Roche. L. L. L. Golden, ed.

Saturday Review of the Society. 1:41-4. Ap. '73. Can the businessman meet our social needs? [debate] P. F. Drucker and E. K. Hamilton.

Science. 168:452-5. Ap. 24, '70. Campaign GM: corporation critics seek support of universities. L. J. Carter.

Science. 171:463-6. F. 5, '71. Corporate responsibility: group rates company social performance. Constance Holden.

Southwestern Law Journal. 25:667-96. '71. Toward a general theory of social responsibility for business. J. F. Lewis.

Spectator (London). 226:617. N. 10, '73. Company (and directors') reform. Nicholas Davenport.

Spectator (London). 227:715. Je. 8, '74. Worker participation in companies. Nicholas Davenport.

Stanford Law Review. 21:248-92. '69. Fact and legal theory: shareholders, managers, and corporate social responsibility. J. A. C. Hetherington.

Time. 95:94-6. My. 11, '70. Corporation becomes target.

Time. 96:62-8. Jl. 20, '70. Executive as social activist.

Time. 98:55-6. Jl. 12, '71. Business and society: responsibility beyond profit.

Time. 100:85-6. O. 16, '72. Women on the board.

Time. 101:25-6. Ja. 22, '73. The thalidomide affair: settlements offered by Distillers Company, Ltd.

Time. 102:74. D. 10, '73. The corporation [review of TV program]. Richard Schickel.

Time. 103:71. Ja. 21, '74. Superbankers in control.

Time. 103:22-4+. F. 18, '74. Exxon: testing the international tiger.

*Time. 103:76-7. F. 18, '74. Madam executive.

U.S. News & World Report. 70:91-3. Ap. 12, '71. American business is plainly in trouble. J. M. Roche.

U.S. News & World Report. 70:52-4. Ap. 26, '71. Business takes on its critics.

*U.S. News & World Report. 74:64-6. My. 21, '73. Why "multinationals" are under fire at home, abroad.

Wake Forest Law Review. 9:463-502. D. '73. Remedies for the abuse of corporate status. H. L. Oleck.

Wall Street Journal. p 14. F. 10, '71. When businessmen turn radical. W. E. Blundell.

Wall Street Journal. p 8. My. 21, '71. Memo to GM: why not fight back? Jeffrey St. John.

*Wall Street Journal. p 1+. O. 26, '71. For many corporations social responsibility is now a major concern. C. N. Stabler.

Wall Street Journal. p 1+. Ag. 9, '72. Losing cause: do-good mutual funds find customers rare, profits elusive indeed: they buy stock in concerns with "social conscience," hope to influence policies. Les Gapay.

Wall Street Journal. p. 10. D. 21, '72. Business must perform better. David Rockefeller.

Wall Street Journal. p 1+. Ap. 19, '73. Many critics charge multinational firms create money crisis: corporate currency moves are cited but companies call tactics "defensive"; a warning to the peasants. C. N. Stabler.

Wall Street Journal. p 16. Ja. 17, '74. The credibility of corporations. Irving Kristol.
*Wall Street Journal. p 14. F. 14, '74. The corporation and the dinosaur. Irving Kristol.